S0-EPT-437

On Your Own

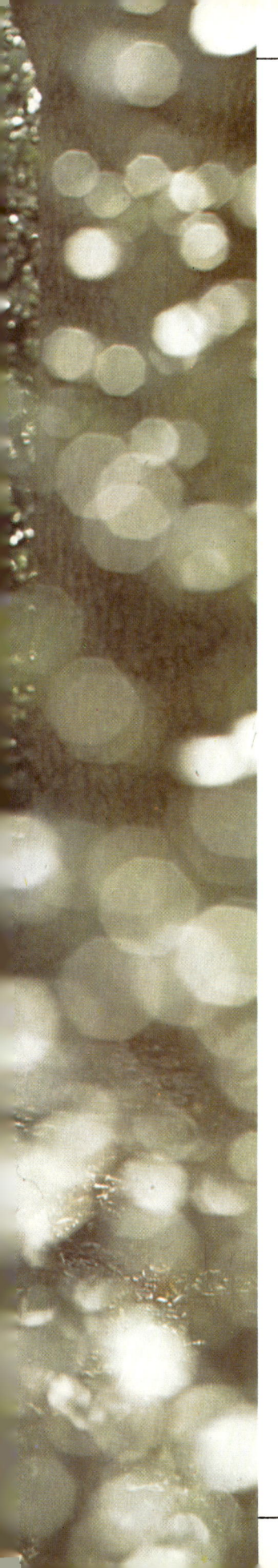

WOMAN ALIVE

On Your Own

by Ann Armstrong

Aldus Books London

Series Coordinator: John Mason
Design Director: Guenther Radtke
Picture Editor: Peter Cook
Editor: Ann Craig
Copy Editor: Mitzi Bales
Research: Elizabeth Lake
　　　　　Sarah Waters
Consultants: Beppie Harrison
　　　　　　Jo Sandilands

Copyright © Aldus Books Limited,
London, 1974
Library of Congress Catalog Card
No. 72-85024
Printed and bound in Yugoslavia by
Mladinska Knjiga, Ljjublana

Contents

For many of us, the world outside married life looks bleak and bewildering. How does a woman cope with the challenges of living alone? This book is not only for the woman who is now on her own. It is also for the woman who wonders how she would manage if she had to be on her own, and for the woman who wants to help someone close to her who is newly alone. Its aim is to provide encouragement and sound advice on the emotional and practical issues that face a woman alone: love and friendship, work and money, day care and single parenthood, decision-making and remarriage—even the special problem of having to "hold the fort" while a husband is away from home.

	The Single Woman: Picture Essay	6
1	Not One Half, One Whole	17
2	When There Are Children	29
3	Finding the Right Job	42
4	Juggling Two Roles	59
5	Decisions; Decisions	76
6	Friends of Your Own	90
7	Loving and Being Loved	102
8	Where Are You Going?	117
	Questions and Answers	129
	For Your Bookshelf	144

The Single Woman

The woman who did not choose to marry has been with us through all of history, though she has mostly been pointed out as unusual. Certainly it is true that formerly a single woman had to be a leading figure of some kind in order to get full social acceptance.

Right: Saint Barbara, an early Christian martyr, is revered as a chaste virgin.
Below left: the Queen of Sheba lives in legend as a powerful ruler—and lover.
Below right: Florence Nightingale sacrificed all personal life to her nursing career.

Above center: Elizabeth I, called the "Virgin Queen" because she never married, was one of England's greatest monarchs.

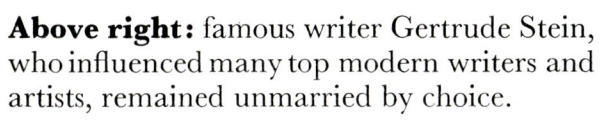

Above right: famous writer Gertrude Stein, who influenced many top modern writers and artists, remained unmarried by choice.

Below: the single woman has often been the butt of unkind jokes. This 19th-century print depicts a spinster as harsh and ugly.

When a Husband Dies

Widowhood is a highly respected status for women, though they may be beset by financial and emotional difficulties. However, many left to make their own way on the death of a husband get a new lease on life.

Right: the Old Testament inspired this painting, showing the widowed Ruth with the man who became her second husband.

Below: there was no widowhood for Hindu women until 150 years ago. Before that, wives were burned with dead husbands.

Above: the Wife of Bath, immortalized by Chaucer in his *Canterbury Tales*, was a lusty woman who was often widowed—but who remarried each time. She had five husbands.

Right: the Victorian widow was bound by a rigid code to certain dress and behavior for a lengthy period of time. Even her jewelry, if she could afford any, had to be made of jet.

Below: Madame Odette Pol-Roger, dubbed a "champagne widow" by the press, is one of a group of French women who successfully run their dead husbands' wine businesses.

When a Marriage Dies

Divorce was long the privilege solely of the powerful or the wealthy and, even among these, could bring some disgrace. Today, divorce is generally easier and more accepted.

Below: in ancient Rome, a married couple had liberal divorce laws available, and marriage could be ended by mutual consent.

Right: for centuries a Church senate—as shown here—had the only and final say on divorce, which was usually by annulment.

Above: King Henry VIII's decision to divorce his wife made him break England away from the Roman Catholic Church.

Above: marriage for Sophia Loren and Carlo Ponti was difficult because even Ponti could not get a divorce in his native Italy.

Above: the 18th-century scandal involving the Duchess of Kingston, pictured here, showed how wealth could buy divorce.

Right: this quickie divorce bureau in Mexico is an extreme example of how easy it is to get in and out of marriage these days.

Women Without Men

There are times when women must live entirely without men—sometimes by choice, but often by misfortune, or social pressure.

Right: an old drawing shows Franciscan nuns, called Poor Clares, singing in the choir in their manless world of religious devotion.

Below: their men have gone off to war—and these ladies of medieval days have been locked up in a tower to assure their chastity.

Above: women in prison are away from all company of men. This illustration shows 19th-century prisoners under surveillance.

Above: this beggar woman with an infant to care for is symbolic of the tragic hard times that a poor widow may find herself in.

Right: the woman cruelly left by a lover—that is the legend of Ariadne, deserted on an island by the man whose life she had saved.

Below: even today in England and elsewhere, girls are kept entirely separate from boys during the school years before college.

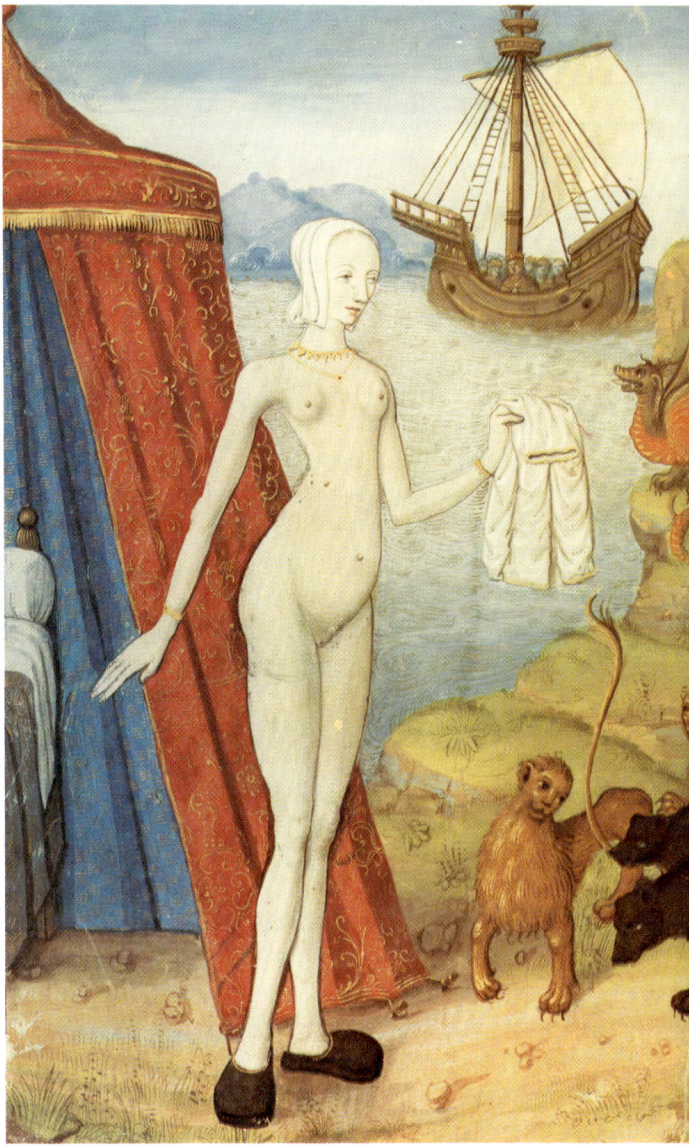

To Marry or Not?

The nature of marriage has changed with the years, and woman's position within it has largely improved. Still, today, the institution of marriage is under question, and many women deliberately choose to stay single.

Below: the romance and expected bliss of marriage is the idea conveyed in this portrait of newlyweds, done in the late 15th century.

Above: marriages of children were often common among royalty. These youngsters became England's William III and Mary.

Above left: the English artist Hogarth satirizes a marriage made for economic gain, in which the prospective couple has no say.

Above: marriage for life was the key to family life in the 19th century. Here is depicted a silver wedding celebration.

Below: the Victorian governess—that overworked, unappreciated single woman—was almost barred from marriage by her job.

Below right: the fortunate modern girl can freely choose to live her life as she wants to—and marriage may or may not enter into it.

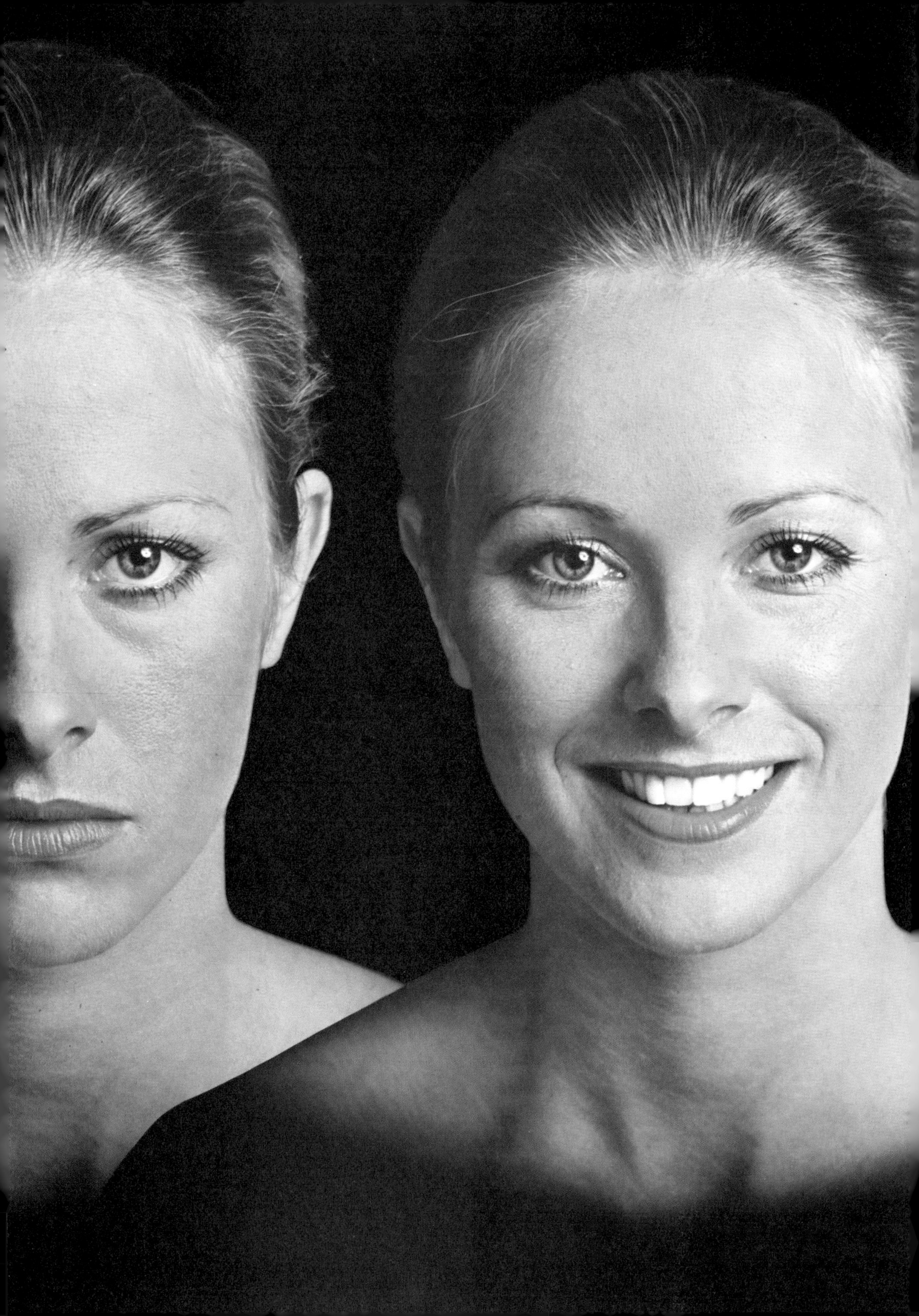

Not One Half, One Whole

1

Gone are the days when a single woman lived in the background of life as a half-being—either a dependent on her family, or an underling servant. Today the woman alone is a complete person, with a place in society.

Chris Irwin, 29, is a divorcee with two small sons to bring up. When she and her husband decided to end their stormy marriage three years ago, Chris's first reaction was one of relief. But once the divorce had gone through, she was gripped by a feeling of stark terror. Their small suburban house had been made over to her, but now she had to make the payments on it—and her child-support allowance was just enough to cover the cost of day and after-school care for the kids while she was at work. Today, her financial position is a precarious one, and juggling the roles of working mother, decision maker, and single woman presents problems. But Chris has found that she can get along all right, and, although she sighs for the days when she didn't have so many responsibilities, is still convinced that the divorce was the right decision for everyone concerned.

Carla Schaefer feels differently about her divorce. She was 44 when, seemingly out of the blue, her husband announced that he wanted to marry another woman. Carla didn't contest the divorce he asked for, but the experience was shattering. For months afterward, she was tormented by bitter despair. It was only at the urging of her college-age daughters that she finally decided to pull herself together, and begin a new life. She moved into an apartment in the city, and, using a skill she had always regarded as a mere hobby, found a job with an interior decorating firm. Today, though she still finds it hard to see herself as a career woman, she enjoys her work, and has even begun to revel a little in her new-found ability to make her own way in the world.

Peggy Bloom, like Carla, also experienced

the shock of finding herself alone in her middle years. For Peggy, however, it was not divorce, but the untimely death of her husband that cut her adrift from the life she had known. When she became a widow at 57, she felt lost and bewildered. Though her friends and family were a great source of comfort and support during the first few agonizing months of her bereavement, there inevitably came a time when Peggy had to face the reality of being alone. The house felt terribly empty, and she contemplated moving to be nearer her grandchildren. But she was reluctant to leave the community she had been a part of for so many years. What was she to do? Talking over her quandry with a neighbor one day, it suddenly struck her that she could bring children into her own home by setting up a small neighborhood day-care center for the children of working mothers. And that's just what she did, with the help of another widowed friend who shares her love of children, and her need for an active and constructive life.

Pat Rossi might secretly envy all three women described above, despite the upheavals they have experienced. Why? Simply because Pat herself has never married. A trim brunette of 36, she has worked for the past 12 years with a large advertising agency, and is well on her way to a managerial position. But despite her success at work, Pat has often had the feeling that she has somehow failed the course by not becoming "Mrs." somewhere along the line. Recently, however, she has taken a new look at herself and her life. "Supposing I don't get married," she says now. "Will that make me any less of a person? What counts is what I do with what I have, here and now, married or not." What this means for Pat is that she has stopped brooding obsessively about her single state, and stopped exhausting herself with work as a way of escaping from it. Among other things, she took her first full-length, solo vacation this year—not with the desperate aim of finding a mate, but simply to unwind, enjoy herself, and learn a little more about the world. She has also begun giving serious

Single, widowed, divorced. Women on their own often learn they can do more than just get along —they find they can build full and happy lives. Above: over 30 and willing to say so, Monika is unmarried—and is enjoying the life she leads.

thought to adopting a child. Whether she does so or not, the fact remains that for the first time, she is thinking of herself as a whole person—not just an incompleted half—with much to give, and a meaningful future to give it in.

Chris and Carla, Peggy and Pat: these four women are neither typical nor atypical of the modern woman alone. They are simply four individuals dealing with four individual problems. Yet they do belong to a growing sisterhood. According to the latest census, no fewer than one out of every three women is currently living alone, or with her dependents. By choice or by chance—through separation or divorce, widowhood, or simply never having said "I do"—30 per cent of the women in America today are on their own. (Just for the record, the figure is 25 per cent for men.)

Very few of us imagine that, after the first few carefree years of youth, we will find ourselves still single, or single again. The agony of divorce, the tragic loss of a loved one, or the idea that one might remain unmarried, have never been easy possibilities to contemplate, especially in a society as couple-oriented as our own. Most of us, in fact, grew up in the firm belief that marriage would provide the basic and continuing framework for our lives, just as it did for our parents, our friends' parents, and most of the other adults

Above: divorced after a long-term second marriage, Valerie Ellis has found satisfaction in her work.
Left: Paula Slater fought her bereavement as a young widow by forming a club for lonely people. Out of the first Solo Club grew hundreds more.

Right: the dream of happiness for most women is still to get married and have the lifelong companionship of a husband, plus the joy of children. This is only natural when we consider that almost all the adults we know as we grow up have a belief in the established institution of marriage.

we knew as children. Certainly the movies and TV programs we saw, the books and magazines we read, all had a way of convincing us that marriage would not only solve our problems, but last us a lifetime. Even more to the point, they left us with the feeling that, over a certain age, an adult woman only counted as an active member of society if she were married. If not—for whatever reason—she seemed invisible.

Well, things are changing—and fast. In part because of the rising tide of divorce, in part because of the powerful new interest in women generated by the liberation movement, the life of the woman alone is beginning to come in for a lot more attention and recognition. Today, the market is flooded with books and articles on the legal and emotional aspects of divorce, on the changing status of the working woman, on the financial complexities of widowhood, on the challenge of single parenthood, and, of course, on the joys and sorrows of the single woman's love life. Each of these is a separate issue, but every woman on her own must deal with more than one of them at a time. So how does she do it? If she solves a problem in one area, does that make for problems in another? How, in fact, does the woman alone manage to get it all together, and what are her most pressing needs?

The basic challenge for most women on their own is the very central one of giving shape and direction to their lives. Put very simply, it's like being faced with the pieces of a complicated jigsaw puzzle, and asked to fit them together in a meaningful and satisfying way. A married couple faces much the same thing when they come to shape their life together. But in their case, there is a finished picture, an established pattern of the desired result, to go by. In the case of the woman on her own, the picture only emerges as she goes along.

For many women, the most critical moment comes with the realization that they *are* alone. This is what's known as the crunch. For a never-married woman, like Pat, the crunch may come when she passes a certain age. It differs from woman to woman, but almost every woman has a kind of deadline age fixed in her own mind, by which time she simply must marry, or begin seriously worrying about herself and her future. For a young divorcee, like Chris, the crunch may come when the legal battles are finally over, and she finds herself facing a host of practical and financial difficulties, while also struggling to get over the hurt and anger that usually accompany a divorce, and dealing with the natural distress of her bewildered children.

For the older divorcee, like Carla, whose children have grown up and left the nest, the crunch may come with a vengeance, particularly if she possesses no other skills than those of wife, mother, and homemaker. The challenge facing her is that of creating a whole new role for herself, both socially and occupationally, and it may require every inch of determination and ingenuity she has to do so. For an older widow, like Peggy, the crunch may come more gradually, as the initial shock and numbness begin to wear off. It is at this point that the terrible lethargy of nothing to do and no one to do it for may set in, and she may be tempted to focus all her energies on her children and grandchildren,

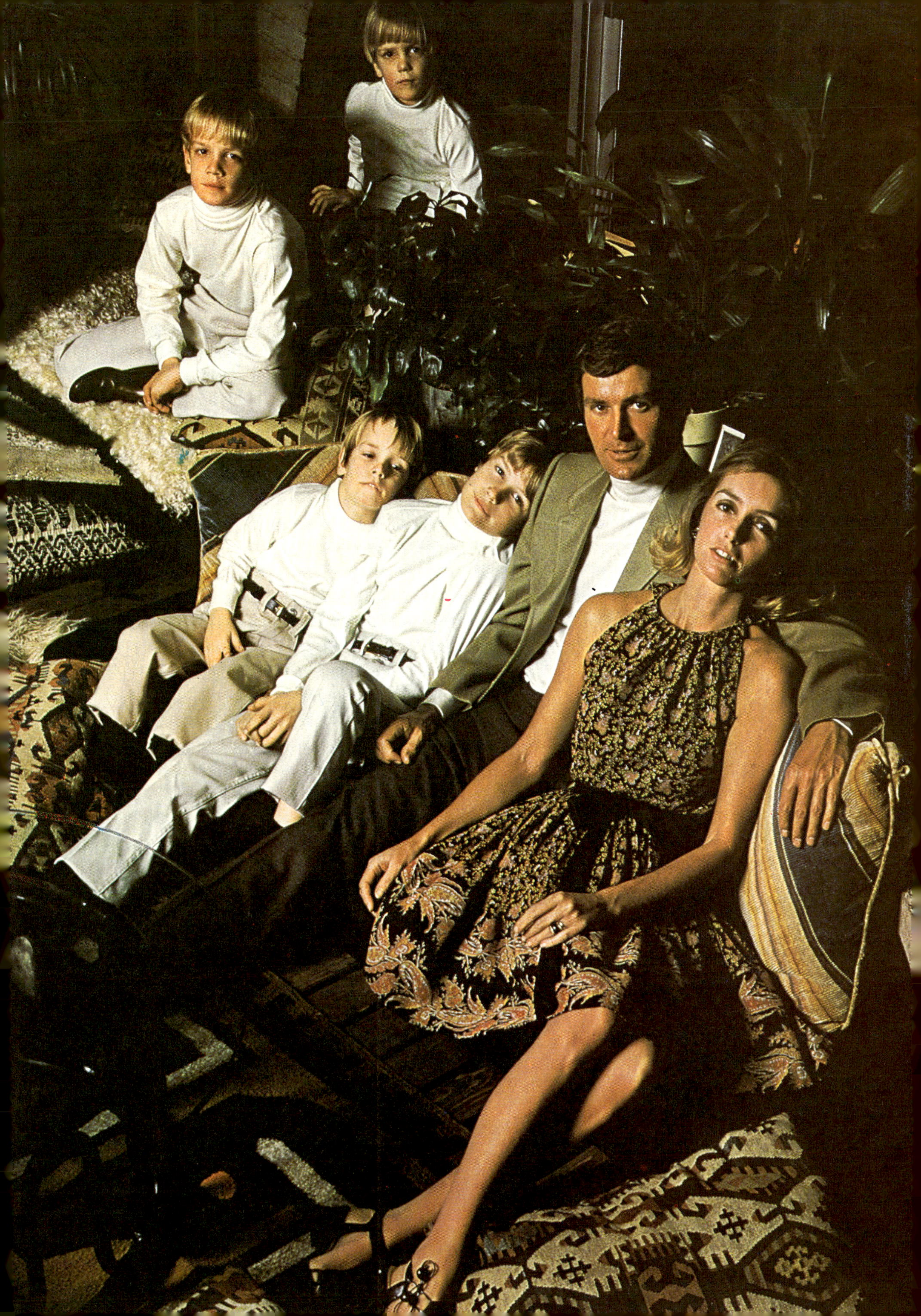

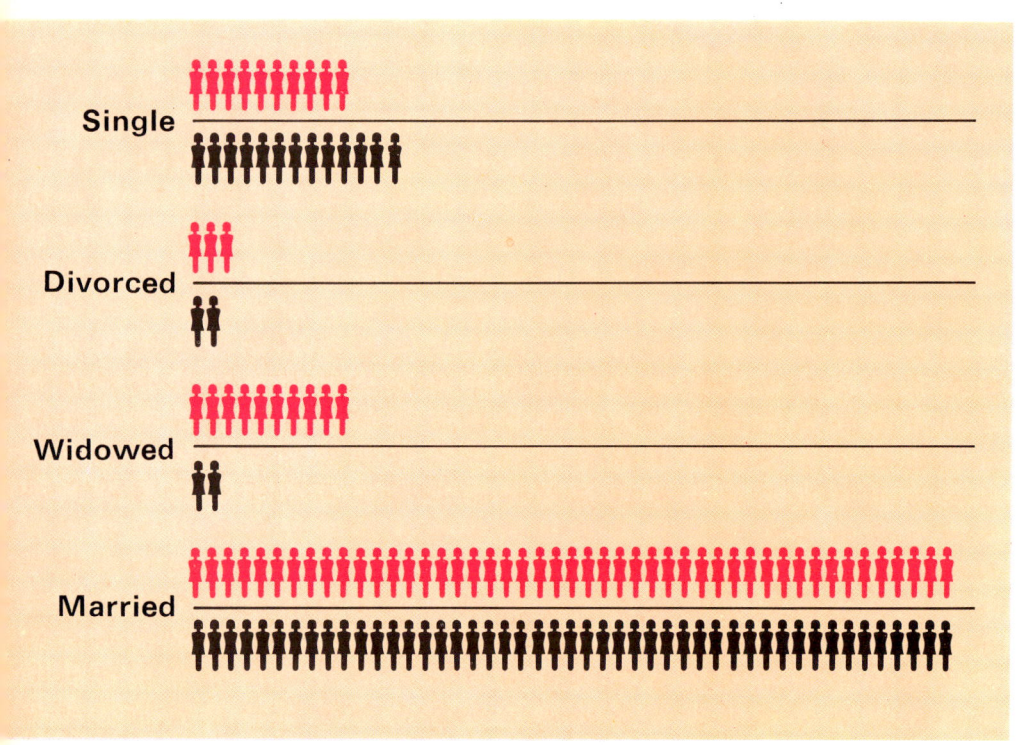

Above: this diagram shows the marital status of men and women over age 18 in the United States for the year 1971. Each figure—women in red, men in black—represents one million. Note that single men outnumber single women. Right: the picture of the single woman as the lonely woman is fast changing.

rather than developing any new interests of her own.

No one would pretend that any of these crises in a woman's life are easy to get through. Each is in its own way harrowing, and brings its own emotional turmoil. There are a few hardy, self-sufficient souls, of course, who ride out the storm with confident equanimity. But the majority experience a tumult of feelings and reactions so new and strange that they may occasionally wonder, "Can this really be me? Can this really be happening?"

One woman may find herself flying off the handle, or weeping inconsolably over little things that never used to matter. Another may find her moods swinging wildly between skittish gaiety and deepest gloom. Yet another may retain her outward calm, but suffer various signs of physical distress, like sleeplessness or blinding headaches. There are some who become temporarily dependent on quantities of food, drink, or cigarettes, and others who—just as temporarily—lose their taste for everything they used to enjoy.

Through it all may run a throbbing current of emotional pain. There may be grief or bitterness, fear or regret, but above all, there is usually an overwhelming sense of aloneness. "What am I going to do now? Who will love and protect me? Can I bear this loneliness?" are the kinds of questions that may haunt the woman newly alone, or newly conscious of being alone.

At such moments, many a woman has felt like a frail craft about to be capsized by the big waves rocking her boat. But, difficult though it may be to grasp at the time, they are all natural, necessary, and weatherable. What never ceases to amaze many people is the way they do manage to come out of their own private storms—not only intact, but more ready for life and living than before. Indeed, in the opinion of most psychologists today, it is precisely such crises that provide the stimulus for personal growth and development. Each of us possesses resources and capabilities we are unaware of, and it often takes a period of crisis for them to emerge. As they do, the personality naturally undergoes an upheaval, but the result is usually much greater personal strength and self-knowledge.

A necessary and intriguing part of the process for many a woman is a kind of personal reappraisal. Who exactly is she? She may, for example, have allowed herself to be defined for many years chiefly in terms of her marital status. Having seen herself through the eyes of her husband and children, family and friends for so long, she may have lost sight of the person she used to be, or wanted to become. While married, it is the easiest thing in the world to go along with other people's image of you, and underplay the kind of qualities and ideas that don't fit. But oddly enough, though a woman may resent having to give up some of her personal likes and dislikes while she is married, she often finds it difficult to reaffirm them when she is not. Suddenly, without another person's views to back her up, she can find it hard to say "*I* like," "*I* prefer," or "*I* believe," with real conviction.

This is a common problem for the woman newly alone, and it's directly related to the greater, underlying problem of feeling somehow less than a whole person. A nagging sense of incompleteness, of being merely one in a world made for twos, can play havoc with a woman's self-image—if she lets it. For here she should remind herself that there are no fewer than 43 million men and women in this country who are on their own right now. Each and every one of them is a complete individual, with his or her own personal tastes and opinions, problems and potentials. Only from an outdated, Noah's Ark point of view are they "outsiders"; there are simply too many of them for that.

Single people, both male and female, are increasing in number. Some of them are remaining single out of choice. Others are remarrying, and passing back into the world they left. But the point remains that the two states of being are becoming more and more equal. It's no longer a question of those who are married ("o.k." types), and those who aren't ("not o.k." types). The stigma of a failed marriage or of remaining unmarried is a thing of the past. Though marriage as a way of life remains as popular as ever, few people would deny that becoming a whole person, capable of growth and change, is every bit as important a goal in life—many people would argue, possibly even more important.

What all this means for the woman alone is that now is the time for her to stand up and be counted. No woman on her own these days need feel that she's some kind of poor relation to the rest of the world. She has plenty of brothers and sisters standing shoulder-to-shoulder with her. They do, however, occupy a different world from that of the married folk, and it's leaving one world and entering the other that often proves the hardest step.

This brings us, of course, to the much-discussed question of the single woman's social status. What happens, socially, after divorce, widowhood, or the relentless process of everyone else you know getting married? Both for the newly single woman, and for the woman who has always been single, there

Joan Bakewell, shown below in a TV studio, made a name in what is still much a man's world—the interview program. Being a divorcee with two children, she necessarily had to combine a career and homemaking. On the right she is seen in her living room, and in a family portrait with her daughter and son.

may be a sense of not belonging. Every woman alone has felt this very keenly at some point. Dropping out of the two-by-two world, whether suddenly or slowly, can be painful, especially if friendships of long standing undergo a cooling down. That they often do is a common experience of both men and women everywhere.

It has become a truism that, hand-in-hand with a change in marital status, goes a change in social relationships. The widow or divorcee usually finds that, for one reason or another—embarrassment or pity, mistrust or simply divided loyalties—some of her friendships melt away. Others, of course, become even stronger. But even their old familiar context has altered, and she may find herself wondering frantically, "Where is the world I used to count on, and belong to?"

For a time, she may rely heavily on some of her married friends, confiding all her personal feelings and troubles to them. But gradually, the differences between her circumstances and theirs, or her chagrin at having divulged so much to them, or their inability to identify wholly with her problems, usually brings such therapeutic confessionals to an end. Though it may have helped her to talk it out, she begins to feel the need for friendships of a more equal nature.

Initially, it may seem to the woman alone that creating a new and satisfying social life for herself is going to be uphill work. Indeed, new friends won't suddenly spring up overnight, like a fairy-tale forest. They need finding and cultivating. But it can't be stressed too much that the building of a new circle of friends and acquaintances is one of the most

Parents Without Partners, an organization in which divorced or widowed parents get together to discuss child rearing, and to make new friends of people in like situation, was formed 16 years ago. This group was taking part in a New York Regional Conference that combined lectures and fun.

important—and gratifying—aspects of being on your own.

Like asserting your own personal tastes and values, finding your feet again socially is related to a deeper issue—that of making decisions. Many a woman on her own has found that the freedom to make major choices —without ever consulting someone else—can be slightly overwhelming at first. This is all the more true in the context of her personal

Real freedom is always a challenge, but it is particularly so for the woman on her own. Nonetheless, she *is* free and, willy-nilly, will find herself positively reveling in it from time to time. Gradually, as she adjusts to her new position, and begins to expand her self-image as a whole person with likes and dislikes, opinions and options of her own, she will begin to find that she can enhance and confirm that image with new friends and social contacts of her own choosing.

There is a world out there that is more flexible, more varied, and sometimes even more supportive and sustaining, than that of married couples. The woman alone may be surprised to discover just how many people there are who aren't married. Up till now, they may have been invisible to her—just as she may suddenly feel herself to be in the world of married people. But they are there. Like her, they are engaged in the baffling and exhilarating process of finding out who they really are, coping with the sometimes frightening freedom to make life decisions that will profoundly affect their futures, dating, and very possibly, seeking remarriage.

So how does the woman alone begin making new and meaningful social contacts of her own? Some suggestions will come in a later chapter—together with ways of getting down to real problem solving—because this is not to be simply a "how-to-catch-a-man-and-be-a-social-butterfly" book. As anyone already on her own knows full well, the life of a single woman—especially if she has children to raise, or if she is older and has never worked—takes a lot of ingenuity. What we propose to offer is fuel for her ingenuity: finding a job and developing a career; solving the day-care problem and being a successful single parent; jockeying her roles as working woman, homemaker, and social animal; making major and minor decisions about housing, insurance, credit buying, and investments; and, of course, never forgetting that she herself—mind and heart and body—must be listened to and cared for with all the attention that a whole person, not just a half, deserves.

relationships, where the options may be a lot more numerous and diverse than they are in any other part of her life. Does she want to embark on a love affair, for example? Or enlarge her circle to include people she might never have met as a married person? The options are wide open, and entirely her own. No longer a little-girl-protected, she must arrange her life as she alone sees fit, and accept responsibility for her decisions.

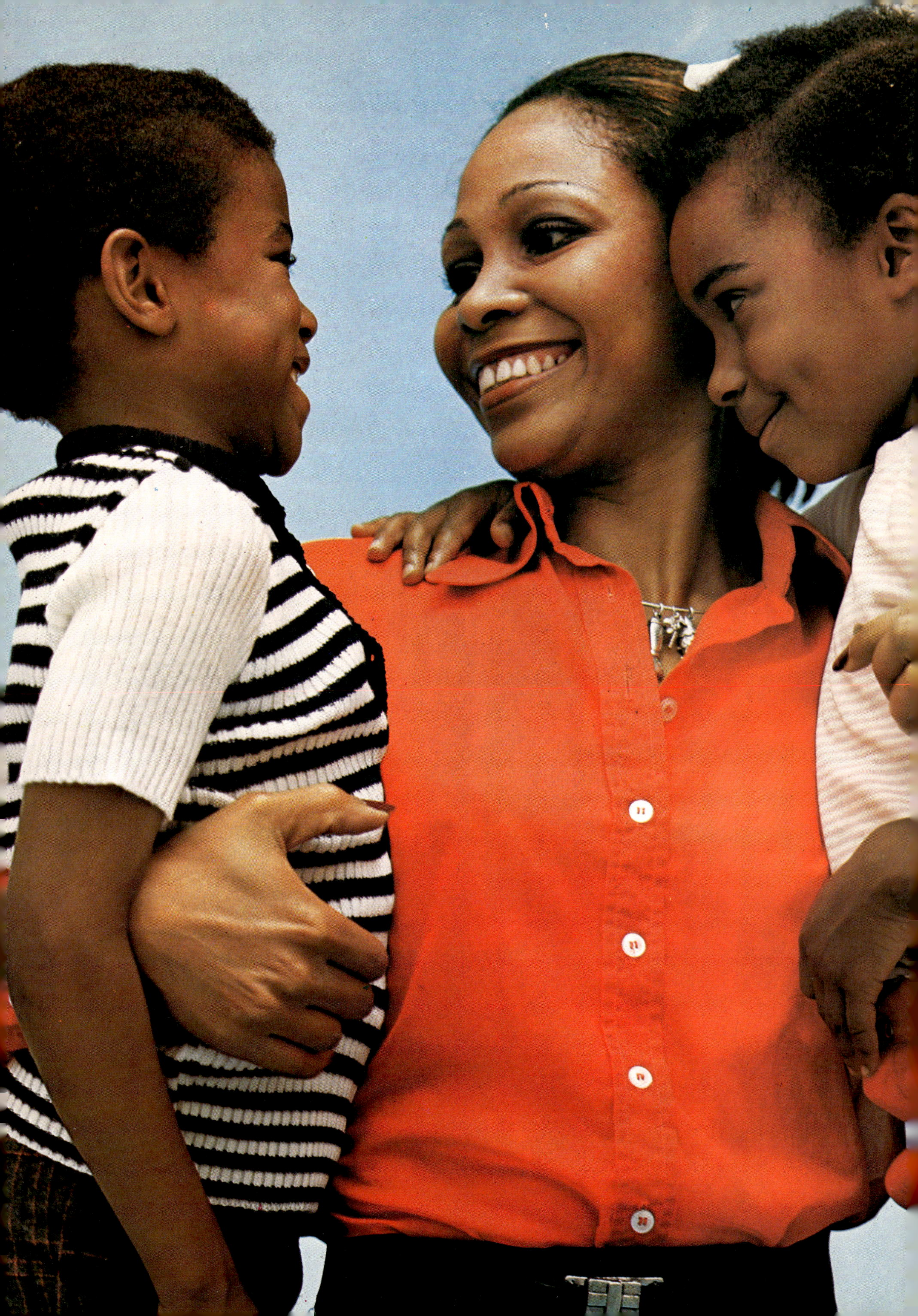

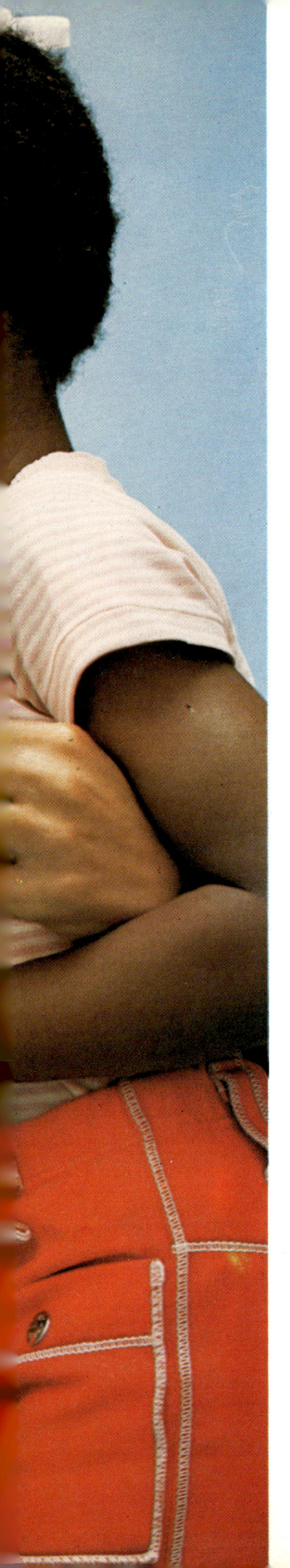

When There Are Children 2

The mother who has to raise her children alone does not have an easy time of it. But it can be a big help to her to understand that her constant love can give them the security they need for happiness as adults.

"Why did Daddy go away?" "Did I do something bad?" "Does he still love us?" "Can't you make him come back?" "Why do I only get to see him on Saturdays?" "What is a divorce?"

"Where did Daddy go when he died?" "Is he up in heaven or down in the ground?" "Can he see what I'm doing now?" "Will you die too?"

These are the kind of troubling questions children ask when divorce or death separates them from their father. None of them is easy for a woman to answer, especially during those first grueling days or weeks after the loss has occurred. Caught up in her own tumult of emotions, she faces the difficult task of explaining to her anxious children why daddy is not going to be with them any more. She knows she must do it, but how?

At moments like these, it is all too easy to give way to your own unhappiness, and be too candid with a child, letting him know exactly how you feel about what's happened. It is even easier, perhaps, to avoid the issue entirely, giving him vague and unsatisfying replies in the belief that you are shielding him from harsh reality. Steering a reasonable course between the two extremes can indeed be a delicate task, but it is not an impossible one if it's done thoughtfully.

A child needs and deserves real answers to his questions—always remembering, of course, that he *is* a child. He cannot handle adult complications any more than he can handle the adult emotions storming around his head. In other words, it is neither wise nor necessary to go into all the ins and outs of the situation with him, as you might with another adult. What he needs are simple, concrete

Right: this young mother is facing one of life's hardest moments—telling her little boy that his Daddy has left them. When a divorce is in the offing, it is usually easier and more comforting to a child if father helps break the news. But a calm way of talking, with plenty of reassurances that both parents still love him, goes a long way to make his situation understandable and bearable.

facts that he can grasp and hang onto. Above all, he needs the reassurance that the adults in his life have the situation—and themselves—well under control, and that, whatever has happened, he is much loved, and in no way to blame. It is also of paramount importance that he feels free to get on with his own life, without worrying that he's responsible for what's going to happen next.

This is not to suggest, however, that he won't pester you with a thousand-and-one questions about the particulars of the new domestic setup. Many a newly single mother has been surprised at her children's preoccupation with such details as whether they will still go to the same school, still see grandma and grandpa, still go to bed at the same time, still keep Rex the dog, still go to the beach in the summertime. "Why are they asking me these things," a woman may wonder, "when something so much deeper is involved?"

The answer should be obvious. Their whole world has been turned upside down, and they want to know if absolutely everything is going to change now that Daddy is gone. A child's whole view of life is based on familiar domestic routines, and he is naturally anxious about how the new situation is going to affect them—and him. When something so radical as the loss of a parent occurs, he wants to know, often in minute detail, exactly how things are going to be from now on. Being sure of these things can give him a large measure of comfort while he struggles to accept the harsh fact of his father's absence.

Putting across this fact—and what it means—is often the toughest hurdle faced by a young widow or divorcee. How to combine gentleness with honesty, simplicity with truth? When a divorce is still in the offing, the problem of breaking the news to the children can sometimes be shared by both parents. But it often happens that the final decision is a sudden one, and breaking the news is left to the mother. As in the case of a widow, telling the children becomes her sole responsibility.

The best approach for a woman in this

position is a direct and straightforward one, as uncolored by her own emotions as possible. "I have some very sad news for you," she may begin. "Your Daddy and I are going to start living separately. We are not going to be married anymore, but are going to be divorced. That means that he will be living in another place, and have his own life apart from us, though you will still see him as often as possible. We know that this decision will hurt and upset you, and we are terribly sorry about it because we both love you so very much. You have brought each of us great happiness, and we don't like having to hurt you in any way. But you must remember that Daddy and Mommy are grownups, with grownup problems to solve. This was a very hard decision for us to make, but we felt it was the best solution to our problems together. Always remember, however, how much we both love you, and please feel free to ask me anything you want to know about when you will see Daddy, and how things are going to be from now on."

They may ask you to go through it all again, and you will, rephrasing it to deal more fully with what seems to worry them most. Be sure to stress how much they are loved, and that they, as children, are—and always were—powerless to affect this adult decision in any way. Many psychologists have pointed out how easy it can be for children to feel that they are somehow responsible for the breakup. This is particularly the case with small boys. Because they may secretly have wished that their father would go away so that they could have mommy all to themselves, they can feel extremely guilty. With a child's unrealistic ideas of his own powers, it is quite possible for him to believe that mere wishful thinking can produce frightening results.

Something of the same guilt feelings may plague the child whose father has suddenly died. Again, in breaking the news to him, the young widow must be forthright about what has happened. Though in her case she need not shield the child from her natural feelings of grief, she must be careful not to let them seem overwhelming. Her child needs the reassurance of her strength at this time.

"Something very sad has happened to us," she may begin. "Daddy has had a heart attack (or was in an accident, or couldn't be helped by the operation, etc.) and he died last night. I know it's difficult to understand just what this means, but very simply, it means that he won't be able to be with us anymore—not because he didn't want to, but because his body wasn't able to go on living. We will all miss him very, very much, but

Above: the period of your own greatest grief—the death of your husband—creates an added problem of how to talk about it with your children. It is made somewhat easier if you've had some kind of general talk about death previously. That occasion may arise naturally when a pet dies, or your child asks about a dead animal.

32

we will remember all the happy times we had together, and those memories will stay with us always. Even so, both you and I will feel very unhappy about his not being here sometimes, and I want you to feel that you can cry whenever you need to. But don't feel that you must be unhappy all the time. Daddy would want you to go on running and playing whenever you feel like it, just as before. And, if anything at all is troubling you, please come and ask me about it. I'll always be ready to listen and try to answer any questions you have."

How you interpret and clarify a child's ideas about death depends, of course, to a large extent on your own beliefs. But however you deal with his questions—whether it be with the reassurance that Daddy's spirit is now with God, or that you do not know whether a person's spirit lives after him except in the minds and hearts of the people who loved him—remember that a child may be concerned with certain concrete questions that might never have occurred to you. For example, when he travels by plane, will he look for Daddy in the clouds? Or, when he sees a Dracula horror movie, will he imagine that Daddy, too, is simply asleep in his coffin? The important thing is to pick up any detail that might be troubling him, and to allay whatever fears or confusions he may have.

Should a child be allowed to go to the

funeral, or be present at the burial? The answers depend largely on his age. If he is a toddler, for example, probably not; if he is a teenager, yes, of course. But what about the in-betweens? The wisest course, in the experience of many young widows, seems to be that of having the children with them at the memorial service, but without the casket on view. It helps if the memorial service is based on things they know—familiar Bible passages and hymns, for example. The presence of friends and family, both at the service and afterward in their home, provides reassurance and affirmation of the loving support of others, and helps them grasp the meaning of what has happened.

How will a child react, either to the death of his father, or to his parents' divorce? His response, in the months that follow, will depend as much on his own particular temperament as upon his age and the circumstances surrounding the loss. Typical reactions can include anything from disbelief and silent withdrawal to inconsolable tears and frightening nightmares; from complete listlessness to frantic and even destructive activity; from spells of infantile regression to a new and inappropriately adult attitude. Any and all of these reactions are perfectly natural; they are a child's way of expressing his profound distress over what has happened. But how does a mother deal with them? The answer lies in her ability to understand and interpret his feelings, and, at the same time, to provide the reassurance that she is strong enough for both of them. For, if he cannot believe in her strength, how will he ever come to believe in his own?

Above: *Little Lord Fauntleroy*, a children's book of the last century, tells how a little boy has to bear the burden as "head of household" on his father's death. This, of course, leaves him no time for the carefree pleasures of childhood. Right: children need to run free. They cannot be expected to act as a stand-in for a missing parent.

She must remember that whatever he is feeling—be it rage or grief or panic—may be frightening him by its very power. He needs to know that she understands how unhappy he is; that she is ready to talk about or listen to whatever is troubling him; and, above all, that she cares too much about him to let him hurt himself or others.

There are a number of obvious—and not so obvious—pitfalls for the single mother during the first year of her being alone. Perhaps the most obvious of these is to become overprotective. Feeling guilty that her child has been put through the trauma of divorce, say, she may vow to make it all up to him by keeping him safe from any hurt or harm. Of course, he does need special love, comfort, and security at first; but if she keeps on swaddling him, she may end by clipping his wings. She must steel herself to discipline him when he is naughty, and allow him to take all those little chances children always do as they take their first steps toward independence.

This is as important for her as it is for her child. It is all too easy in these first few months to form an all-encompassing bond with one's children, shutting out the rest of the world, and creating a mutual dependence that helps neither you nor them. Children are more sensitive than any radar screen, and can pick up even your innermost feelings. The important thing is not to let them overreact to your emotions. Resist, with might and main, the temptation to let them become mother's little confidants, sympathizers, or defenders. It is all right for them to know that you are lonely and unhappy sometimes, but it is not all right for them to feel that they must make up for what is missing in your life by playing the role of the missing parent. They must feel free to be what they are—children—and trust you to be what you are, an adult capable of handling herself—and them—in life's new situation.

In this connection, it is also important to insist on your right to privacy, and equally, upon your right to a social life of your own. It is not a good idea, for example, to allow either a boy or a girl, however young, to sleep in your bed with you, comforting though it might be. Sharing a bed is for mothers and daddies, not mothers and children. The same goes for your life as a social being. Force yourself, if you have to, to keep up your old contacts, and make new ones. Go out, and have friends over. The children must see that you and your time do not belong solely to them. If they are allowed to get this impression early, their whole security will be threatened every time they have to share you with someone else.

Another common pitfall is to be too honest with the children concerning your feelings about their father. When a divorce has occurred, particularly if there has been a great deal of hurt and anger on both sides, it is all too easy to say what you really think. But however the children's father may have behaved—or may still be behaving—he is their father, and it can do them nothing but harm to hear you tear him down.

This brings us to one of the greatest problems that goes with a divorce: a father's visiting rights. To begin with, there is the whole issue of the children's divided loyalties.

Uncertain about whether it is possible to love and be fair to both parents, they may fall into the trap of equalizing things by tale-telling. ("Daddy had this strange lady with him when we went to the park on Saturday." "Daddy gave me two dollars and let me stay up till midnight." "Daddy didn't like it that you left us with Joanne when you went away last weekend.")

Left: a happy trip to the zoo on father's visiting day, or a quiet story time with mother at home —the child of divorced parents can remain happily close to both, even if activities are separate.

Right: a movie of the 1950's, *Count Your Blessings,* made a comedy situation out of a child who kept his parents from a reconciliation because he liked having two households. This still from the film shows the parents in battle over the child. In their zeal to make things up to their children, divorced parents sometimes forget that a child might try to play one against the other.

who just fades away. He begins by coming regularly to visit the kids, then becomes more and more irregular, missing more and more of his rightful opportunities to see them. This can be a cruel disappointment for your children, who look forward eagerly to his visits, and cannot understand why he does not come. If, in addition, he fails to answer their letters, forgets their birthdays, and is unavailable at Christmas, it is natural for them to feel utterly bewildered and rejected. Your own feelings about all this are, just as naturally, ones of anger and bitter resentment. But now is not the time to give way to them. Your children need your support and reassurance in this matter, not a thunderbolt of fury at the way they're being treated by their father.

If this kind of thing starts happening, discourage it fast, and firmly. What they do with their father is privileged information. If they insist on telling you, listen, but ask no searching questions, and refrain from making criticisms of him. This may be difficult, but it will help them see that their relationship with their father is separate from their relationship with you, and that the two must not be brought in conflict with one another. In some instances, it may be necessary to consult with the children's father on matters of discipline, and even to ask for his cooperation in maintaining certain standards. In all but the rarest cases, however, there is no cause to obtain a court order preventing him from seeing them.

A far more common complaint among divorced mothers is the problem of the father

With all the calm and understanding you can muster, explain that their daddy does indeed still love them, but is unable at this time to be with them as often as he'd like to be. Remind them, if he is failing to answer letters or send birthday gifts, that he always did have a bad memory for dates, and has never been too good at writing letters. If it begins to look as though he's disappeared from the scene altogether, it may be the wisest and gentlest course to say simply that you yourself do not completely understand his behavior, but that one day, perhaps both you and they will understand it better. Perhaps too, when they are grownups themselves, they will be able to get together with their father and talk with him about it.

In the complete, or near-complete, absence of a father, is it possible for children to grow up with a healthy attitude toward sex and marriage? The answer to this troubling question is "yes," with one qualification. No relationship of yours—whether with a male friend or relative, with a lover, or even with a new husband—will completely make up to them for the absence of their true father. In other words, no other male-female relationship, platonic or romantic, of which you are a part, will include them in the same way as your relationship with their father. A marriage into which a child is born has already become a complex mixture of sexuality and affection, respect and comfortable familiarity. This is a picture of man and woman together that no other relationship can exactly reproduce.

All is not lost, however. Remember that it can be far more damaging for a child to experience a hostile and unsuccessful relationship between two parents than to grow up with a single, happier parent. Remember too, that in showing care to develop in your child the attributes of trust and independence, self-respect and concern for others, you are laying the groundwork for a mature personality capable of filling in this one gap in his experience. The child of a single-parent home often possesses a flexibility, an inner strength, and a depth of understanding that make solving adult problems easier for him than for others. If you have helped him develop these qualities, he is well on his way to being a mature adult.

In the meantime, what about providing him with a father-figure? It is obviously important, for both boys and girls, to have a man in their lives to identify with, or relate to. Such a man can bring out, even in minor

A mother alone must try to bring a father figure into her children's life, especially for boys. If there is no doting grandfather around, as below, there is usually some concerned male who will be a kind of substitute, be it a scoutmaster, as at left, a fatherly neighbor, or even a male baby sitter.

ways, the kind of healthy spectrum of responses they might have had to their real father. If possible, he should even be a little bit like their father. They may have inherited many admirable qualities of their father that you, as a different personality, find it hard to draw out and develop. A man who has these qualities might be able to help.

The trouble is, good father-figures are not easily come by. If a woman is lucky, she will have some stable, reliable male relative who can fill this role—one of the children's grandfathers, for example, or a brother, brother-in-law, or uncle. But many women have no such ideal person nearby who can become a permanent fixture in their children's lives—and the point is that the father-figure must be a fairly permanent fixture, someone who can visit often, be relied upon in emergencies, and exemplify what it is to be a grownup man without being a threat to the family setup. For, as both the experts and simple common sense make clear, a succession of males who are romantically interested in mommy, and who come and go like the seasons, can be more disturbing—again to girls as well as boys—than at all beneficial.

If a woman finds that she has no responsible, nonthreatening person around to be a father-figure to her children, she might do well to investigate other avenues: finding a reliable male baby sitter, for example; or joining Parents Without Partners, which runs children's outings with single fathers and mothers joining forces to supervise the kids; or establishing a relationship with a couple whose male half is a good father to his own children, and is willing to take others on for outings or just general roughhousing. Sports and hobby activities run by both men and women are another thing to try. Among these are swimming or boating classes, pottery or carpentry classes, summer camps, scout groups, etc.

If all else fails, the single mother must simply rely on her own good sense—and the innate adaptability and resilience of her children—to see them through their fatherless years, and into the beginnings of adulthood. Growing up without a father, even without a father substitute, is not, and never has been, an unsurmountable handicap. Already we are

That growing up without father is not necessarily a handicap is proved by the illustrious career of George Washington, whose widowed mother had to raise him alone. It was she who, in the painting on the left, persuaded him not to go to sea. If he had not taken her advice, perhaps he wouldn't have become the great political figure known as the "father of his country", as he is depicted on the right.

surrounded by thousands of men and women from one-parent homes who demonstrate, by their own lives, that it is possible to grow up whole and healthy.

Certainly, it isn't easy to bring up children single-handedly. You have no one to consult, no one to back you up, no one to praise you for a job well done. You and you alone command the ship, and all who sail in it. It's a tough job because it demands so much patience and forbearance, self-control and foresight. Hardest of all may be laying down the law and setting standards. But the authority is yours, by virtue of the responsibilities you have assumed, and there is no one to cross you up in the establishment of values and codes of behavior. That is one of the advantages of being a single parent. Another is the joy of watching your care and concern bear fruit in children you can be proud of. Perhaps the greatest of all is your pride in yourself: the knowledge that you are setting your children the finest example possible—that of an adult who has faced a major challenge, and accepted it with courage and resolve.

Finding the Right Job
3

It's a rare woman on her own these days who can afford—either financially or psychologically—not to work. A job is usually an absolute necessity for the younger divorcee or widow, even when she doesn't have children to raise, but especially if she has. Very few divorcees today receive alimony, and what they are granted in child support is either insufficient, or simply not forthcoming. A widow may have been left some money, and also be receiving Social Security; but more often than not, she, too, has insufficient funds to make ends meet. Sheer financial necessity is also why the single woman works. She has to in order to support herself, and sometimes an ailing parent as well.

But supposing money were no object, and the woman alone didn't have to work. She would probably still want, and need to, work. Why? The answers are simple, but crucial to her morale and well-being. To begin with, there's the question of who she is, and wants to be. She feels the need to define herself, to sharpen her sense of identity and purpose. She wants to realize her potential, and give shape and direction to her life. But she can't do it in a vacuum. She needs a focus for her energies, a goal to set her sights on, a context in which to achieve recognition. The right job, as many a woman has already discovered, can provide all three.

The single woman with young children to bring up feels these needs just as acutely. But she often feels overwhelmed with guilt about

Women today do not have to be satisfied with the less exciting jobs once described as "women's work". Few fields are now closed to females—as is shown by this trained laboratory technician.

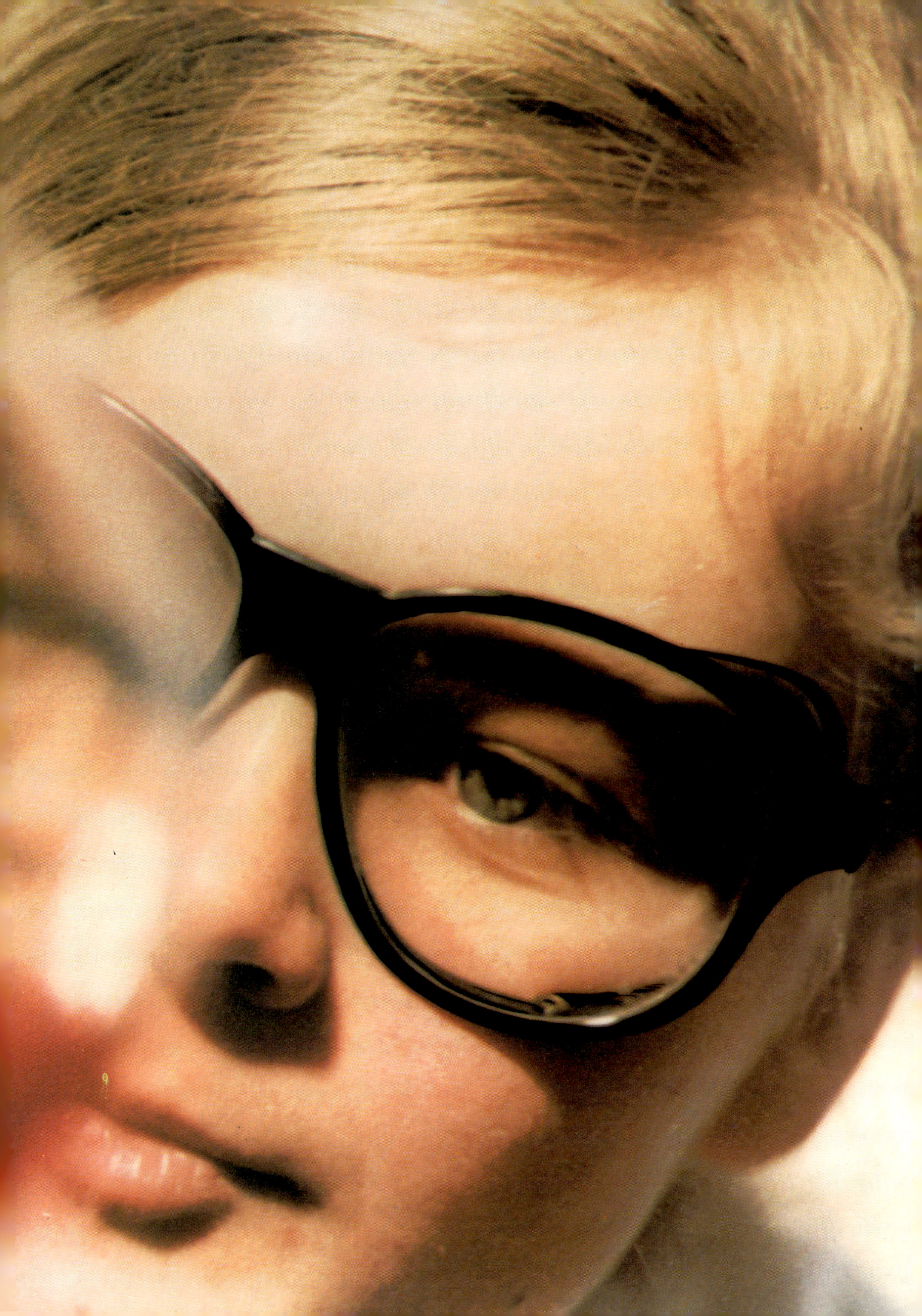

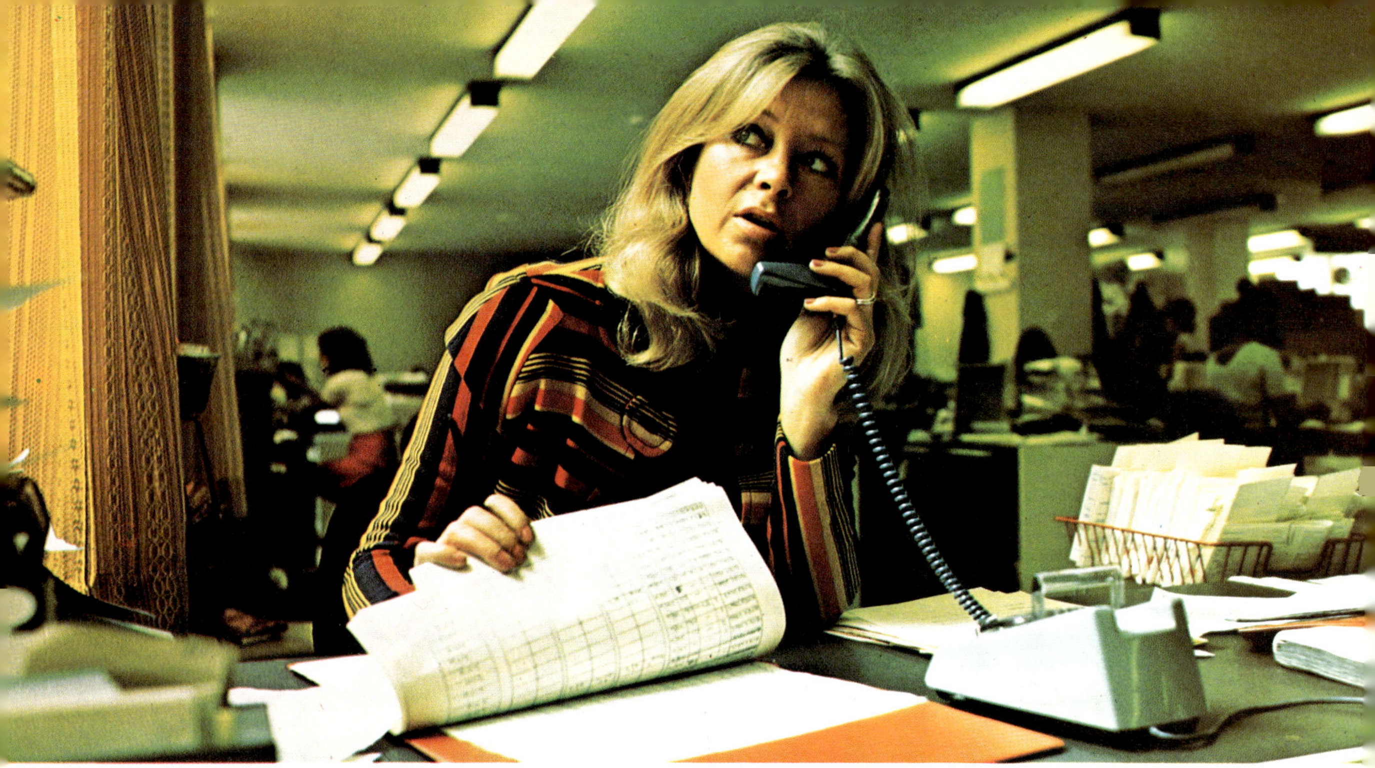

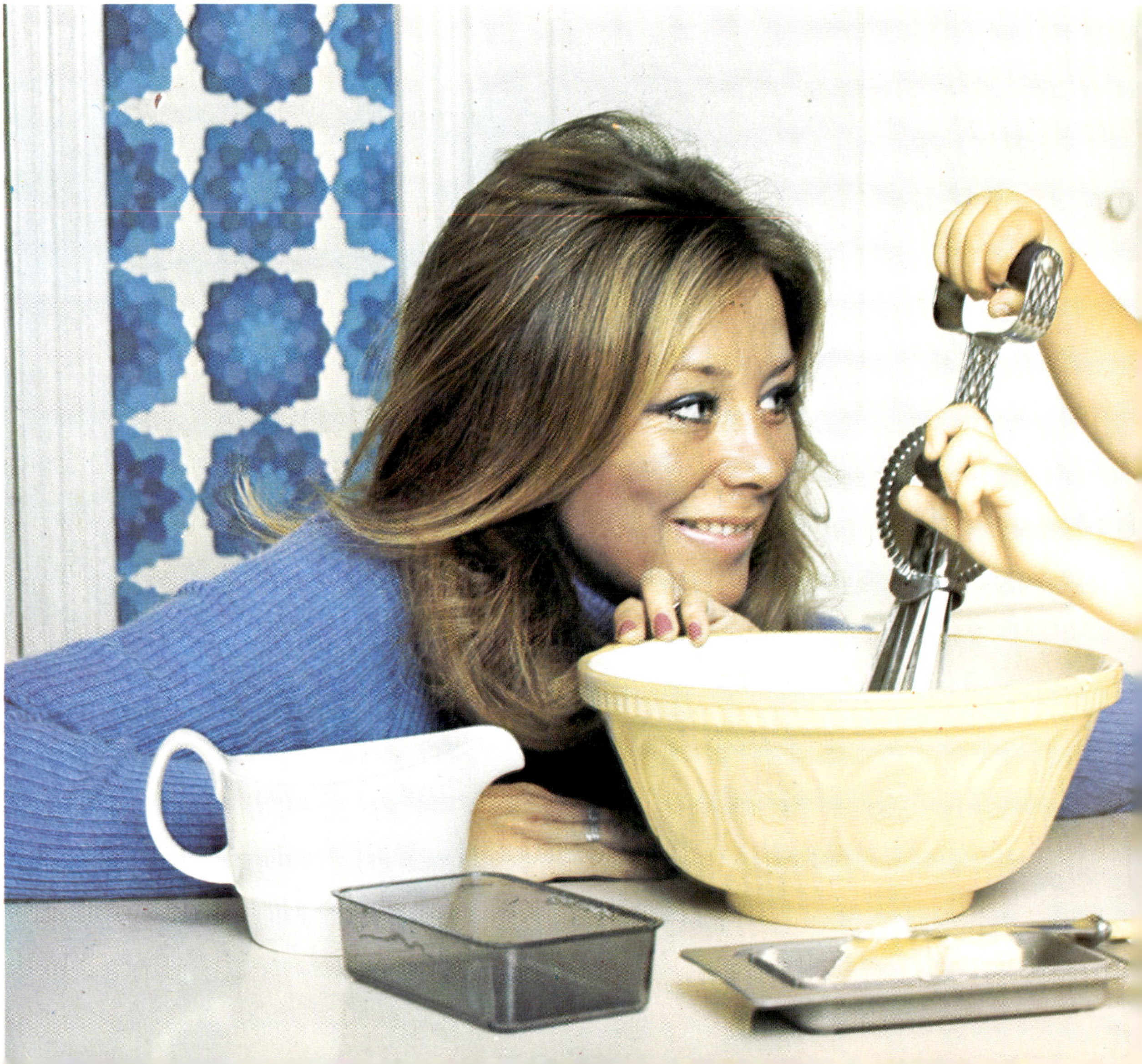

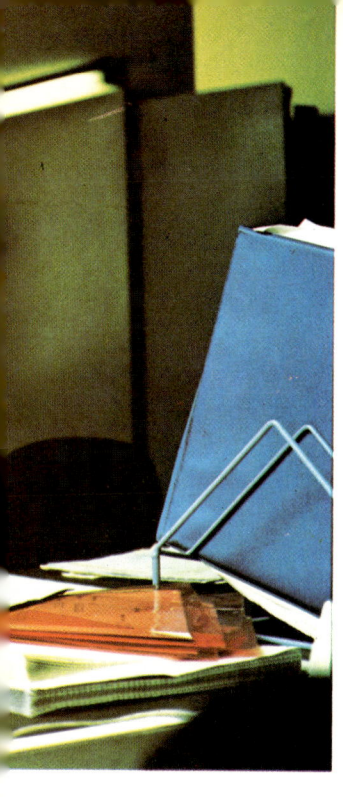

The mother who has an interesting working life, with adult companions, is often a better mother for it. Because she feels more fulfilled as a human being, she can give more of herself to her child in their times together.

having, or choosing, to go out to work. "What will it do to the children?" she asks herself. "What will it do to me? How can I possibly manage two jobs at once?" Certainly no one would deny that the working mother faces a special challenge to her stamina, her ingenuity, and her unique responsibilities as a mother. Just because it is a special challenge, the whole next chapter is devoted to the problems of finding good day-care for the children, and juggling the twin roles of mother and working woman. But for now, let it simply be said that she mustn't allow herself to waste what is precious energy feeling guilty about working, especially if she needs the money. Not only she herself, but her children as well, will ultimately benefit from the companionship of a mother who is happier and more confident in herself because she is finding fulfillment in a job.

For there is more to working than achieving self-definition, recognition, and that all-important paycheck. The woman on her own —whether divorced, widowed or single— needs to stimulate her mind, and find a creative outlet for her skills. She needs the companionship of other adults, and the undeniable satisfaction of being essential to some enterprise larger than herself. Most of all, she needs the kind of schedule and set of demands that give structure to her daily life.

Needing all these things, how does she go about satisfying them with a job that's right for her? Obviously, the single working woman has already begun. But she may need a new beginning if, up until now, she has just been drifting along with the idea that her job is only a temporary fill-in before marriage. Similarly, the divorcee or widow who was working part-time or full-time before her marriage ended, may have simply regarded it as a sort of extra-curricular activity. For each, the time may have come to take a good hard look at the job she has been doing. Is the salary high enough? Is the work itself interesting? Does it challenge her in any way? Are her fellow employees congenial and stimulating? Are there opportunities for advancement? Does her company offer any

45

fringe benefits in the way of life or health insurance, profit sharing plans, etc.? If she finds that her job isn't meeting her needs, she may want to kick over the traces, and start anew.

The woman who is already working—whether or not she is satisfied with her job—is, of course, one step ahead of the woman who is not. For it often happens that a woman suddenly finds that she has to go out to work, or wants to go out to work, for the first time in her life. What can she do? Is she too out of touch, too lacking in experience, or simply too old to enter the job market? Certainly not! Any woman with guts and determination can find a niche for herself in the world of work at practically any age. There are literally thousands of occupations to choose from today, and women are finding a place for themselves in more and more of them. Almost 50 per cent of all the women in America—single, married, separated, divorced, or widowed—are now working, and their median age is a surprising 39.5.

Whether you are already working, have worked, or are looking for a job, there is one major pitfall to be avoided at all costs. That is to rate your abilities and potential so low that you'll take—or keep—any job, however dull and unrewarding it might be. It's true, of course, that a woman can find herself in straits so dire that she must take practically the first thing that comes along just to keep herself and her family going. But ultimately she must demand more of herself and for herself. A job taken in desperation—unless it luckily turns out to be a satisfying one—must not be allowed to snap its jaws on you forever. Like the woman who is reexamining the potentials of the job she has been doing, or the woman who has enough capital to keep herself going while she looks for something that suits her, you must ask yourself: "What would I really like to do?"

For many women, this question can be a real poser. Perhaps half a dozen zany ideas quickly come to mind, and just as quickly cancel themselves out. Obviously, you can't become an airline pilot, a theater director, or

Just a few of the jobs a woman might consider in looking for work: waitress, teacher, lab technician, and computer programmer. If going to school is a problem for you, other jobs you can do besides waitressing include teacher's aide, receptionist, sales person, publicity, and fund raising.

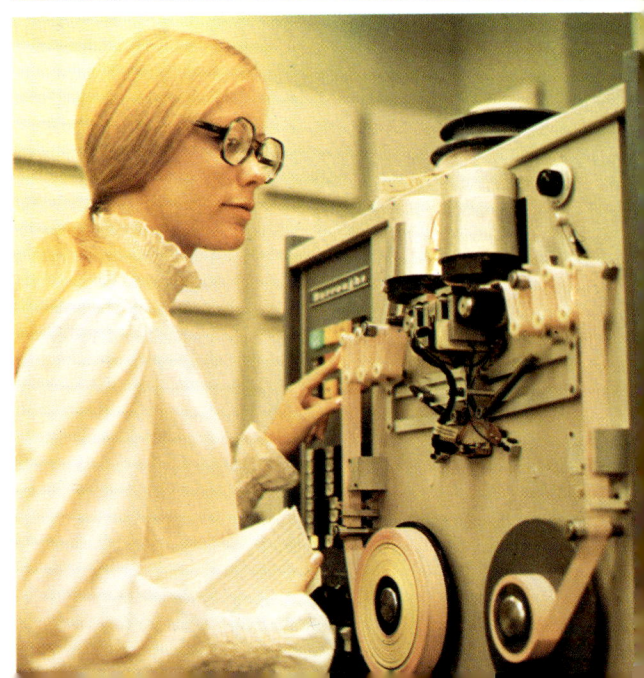

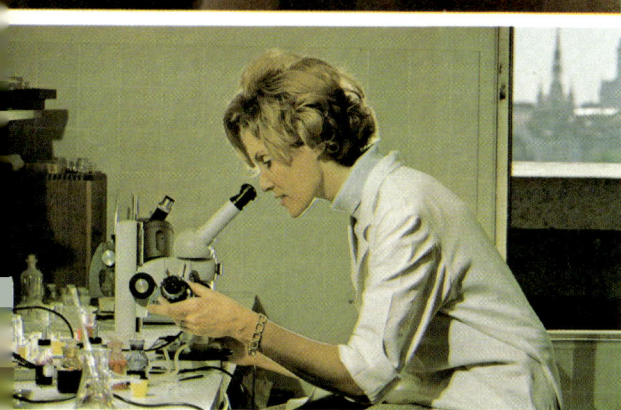

a wizard of high finance at the flick of a switch. There is, however, no reason in the world why you shouldn't use a little imaginative daring when it comes to thinking about what appeals to you. This must, of course, be tempered by your own interests, experience, past training, if any, and capabilities. The trouble is, many women who have never worked before, or who have only done drift-along temporary or part-time jobs, may be totally uncertain about where their real capabilities lie.

If this is your problem, the next step is to seek some good vocational advice. There are many sources for such advice. Perhaps the best are the professional guidance agencies all over the country. The good ones are listed in the *Directory of Vocational Counseling Services*, available at most public libraries, or by writing direct to the American Personnel and Guidance Association, 1605 New Hampshire Avenue N.W., Washington, D.C. The price is about $1.50.

Other helpful sources of professional advice are local college or university guidance centers; community social agencies with job clinics; trade or professional associations in your field of interest; and reputable employment agencies—the kind that take time with their clients, and are experienced at discerning what people have to offer, and what is most likely to suit them.

With career opportunities expanding as rapidly as they are, the important thing becomes finding the right one for you. Perhaps you trained to be a teacher, a nurse, or a librarian before you married, but would now rather be a guidance counselor, a laboratory technician, or a market researcher. Perhaps you know that you could brush up on your typing and shorthand—one woman actually did this by taking "dictation" from radio programs and typing them up—but that when you go back to work as a secretary, you want to make sure you don't always stay a secretary. Possibly you feel particularly handicapped because, as a full-time wife and mother, you've never had a real job. Though you may possess all the determination of the

The Job Market

On these two pages you'll find a varied sampling of the many different kinds of jobs available. The important thing, of course, is to find out what you'd like to do, and then get paid for doing it!

Children

The whole field of education and child care is a natural for you if you've had children of your own.

Public School Teacher
Private School Teacher
Day-Care Center Assistant
Teacher Aide
Babysitter or Housekeeper
School Counselor
School Administrator
School Librarian
School Social Worker
Child Welfare Officer

Publishing and the Applied Arts

If your talents lie in any of the literary or artistic fields, you may well be able to find a job that not only provides an outlet for your creative ability, but also pays you for it. Many of the jobs below require no special training — just a good imagination.

Editor or Copy Editor
Advertising Copy Writer
Literary Agent
Reporter
Photographer
Broadcasting Worker
Commercial Artist
Graphic Designer
Interior Decorator
Set or Costume Designer

Working with People

Almost every job, of course, entails "working with people". But here we mean it in the sense of helping them: providing services, finding solutions to their problems, arranging for their needs to be met. Training is needed for most of these jobs.

Social Worker
Family Service Worker
Family Counselor
Rehabilitation Counselor
Vocational Guidance
  Counselor
Personnel Specialist
Public Relations Officer
Placement Officer
Hotel Receptionist
Office Manager

Health

This is an area in which an interest in science and the welfare of others is important. But most of the jobs listed below do require at least two years of college and one to three years extra training.

Medical Social Worker
Doctor's Receptionist
Practical Nurse
Doctor's Assistant
Dental Hygienist
Laboratory Technician
Dietician or Nutritionist
Speech Therapist
Physical Therapist
Medical Record Librarian

Business

This is the broadest field of all, and includes everything from the most basic office work to the most specialized positions in the fields of money and banking, law and government. The higher you aim, the more training and experience you need.

File Clerk or Typist
Switchboard Operator
Administrative Assistant
Executive Secretary
Office Manager
Market Researcher
Public Accountant
Bank Teller
Bookkeeper or Auditor
Insurance Agent
Civil Servant
Legal Assistant

Buying and Selling

In this job category go a wide variety of jobs that combine business and working with people. Jobs in buying and selling often require no prior training; you simply learn the ropes on the job. What you do need is faith in the product or service you're dealing in, and an ability to size up customer needs.

Salesperson
Retail Buyer
Merchandising Manager
Advertising Copy Writer
Fund Raiser
Travel Agent
Real Estate Agent
Public Relations Officer

woman who wants to switch fields, or use her secretarial talents to move ahead, you may feel that you're starting from scratch because you have no marketable skills. But you have. Never underestimate the kind of abilities and special talents you've developed as a homemaker; they can have real value on the job market.

Perhaps, for example, you have always been especially adept at handling figures and household finances. (How about becoming a CPA or a computer programmer?) Perhaps you have developed an unusually keen eye for house and property values. (What about embarking on a career as a real estate agent?) You may be a superb and imaginative cook. (Could you, perhaps, run a catering service?) Or you may be an accomplished seamstress and decorator, with an expert's eye for fabrics, colors, and styles. (What about going into interior decorating, or becoming a buyer for a department store?)

Your particular gift may have shown itself in your ability to organize family vacations and group outings. (You might become a travel agent, a tour operator, or a public relations person for an airline or hotel.) Or you may have won laurels for your skill in handling committees and projects involving different kinds of people. (What about a job in city government, or as a personnel manager, or administrative coordinator?)

Obviously, if you are the sort of woman who has reveled in child rearing, who possesses those special instincts for handling small people, and who has retained a keen interest in child development, you already have a firm platform to build on. (How about becoming a teacher or a social worker, helping to run a day-care center, or putting your special understanding to work as receptionist to a pediatrician?)

Clearly, special training is required for many of the jobs suggested above. You may quickly discover this when you work out what it is you want to do, and are best suited for. So where do you get the training you need? Occasionally, you can actually get it on the job. Some companies run special trainee programs. In other cases, you simply start out as low man on the totem pole, and work your way up as you gain in experience. But what if the necessary training is not available on the job? The solution to this problem rests partly on your present financial position.

If, for example, you have a little capital, and can afford not to work for a time, you can go back to school. More and more women in their middle years are doing this to prepare themselves for a new career—and, incidentally, enjoying the experience as they never enjoyed their earlier education. If the idea appeals to you, but you are slightly put off by the academic and residence requirements of a traditional four-year degree course, give a thought to attending a community college. Flexible and democratic, such schools offer everything from liberal arts to business and technical programs, and specialize in two-year associate degrees. These degrees can later be cashed in as half the requirement for a bachelor's degree at a more traditional college or university, if you wish.

You may well be one of the many women who have neither the money nor the time required for learning a job. If this is the case, your best bet is to take a "meantime" job, in

For any woman who loves children—especially if she has had some experience in child rearing—teaching can be one of the most rewarding jobs in the world. No one will say it's easy, but most will say it contributes to society in an important way.

your field of interest if possible, and get the extra training you need through evening courses at an adult education center. These centers—operating in grade schools, high schools, community colleges, technical institutes, and Y's—are fast becoming the solution to many people's need for further training, and even degrees. It is not unusual for men and women to spend eight years working toward a bachelor's degree at such centers. But even if a B.A. is not your object, an adult education center can provide the basic or advanced courses you need to qualify for the job you have your heart set on. A fringe benefit of such courses is that they bring you in contact with other like-minded adults. This in itself can be supportive and stimulating.

Let's suppose for the moment, though, that you have the training you need, or that you are looking for a "meantime" job in your field. How do you go about finding it? There are four main avenues to try. First, of course, tell anyone and everyone you know—friends, relatives, neighbors, committee associates, —what you are looking for. It's surprising how often such grapevine contacts can turn up a good job.

Second, scan the want ads in as many papers as you can get hold of. Look for

Central Station, with applicants being shuttled in and out every five minutes. If they're not getting much attention, you probably won't either. Don't bother with it if the agency charges a mysterious "registration fee". Good ones don't charge anything unless, and until, they find you a suitable job. If you have children, keep an eye out for an agency that specializes in finding jobs for working mothers. They know your problems, and are already in touch with the kind of firms that welcome working mothers.

Fourth, try the direct approach. Contact former employers, the trade or professional association in your field, and/or the personnel departments of the organizations you'd like to work for. You'll lose nothing by finding out

Above: she's studying statistics at college and managing the household, too—and she's succeeding at both. Her aim is to be prepared for a good job when she can leave the children to work full time.

reasonable, straightforward job offers, and when you find one or more that appeals to you, phone or write immediately, applying for the job and requesting an appointment for an interview.

Third, seek out a reputable employment agency—more than one, if you can. If you are uncertain about the quality of the agency before you get there, you can check it out fast on arrival. Steer clear if it looks like Grand

what oportunities there are, and you might just strike it lucky.

One aspect of job hunting is preparing a resume. This record of your work experience, education, and qualification serves several purposes. It helps clarify your own thinking about your skills and background. It serves as a business introduction, demonstrating your ability to organize facts, and state what you have to offer. It functions as a record in the files of personnel departments and your employment agency. Most important, it helps to grease the wheels when you have an interview coming up.

What should a resume be like? Basically,

53

something along the lines of the example at right—simple, informative, and accurate. In a way, resumes are a bit like job interviews, though rather more one-sided, of course. In both, you want to appear professional, honest, and personable.

If you're feeling anxious about being interviewed, it may help to remember that much of what you say will not hurt your chances. Indeed, many an interviewer is as new at the game as you are, or such an old hand at it that only the weirdest remark on your part would make a bad impression. For example, many interviews include some standard question about what you consider your greatest weakness. If you answered "impatience," or "a tendency to procrastinate a little," the interviewer probably wouldn't take much notice. If, however, you said, "I don't think I have any weaknesses," or "I never get along with other women," the interviewer certainly would take notice—and possibly offense as well.

There are two other questions you ought to be prepared for in an interview. One is that old standard about why you want the particular job you're applying for. Here's where being professional comes in. Be clear and positive, rather than vague and negative. In other words, it would be better to say, "This is the work I've been trained for and enjoy," or "This is a field I'm eager to enter and gain experience in," rather than something like, "I just adore working with people," or "I can't stand being at home any more, and I've got to earn money somehow."

The other question will apply to you only if you are a working mother. The interviewer often wants to know if you have already made arrangements for your children to be cared for while you're at work. Obviously, if the job is going to be available immediately, it will help a lot if you can honestly answer "yes".

Remember, too, that an interview is an exchange of information. This is your opportunity to find out more about the job: what it entails, the hours and salary, whether there will be opportunities for advancement, the vacation and sick leave regulations, what

Right: a resume is the businesslike and accepted way to introduce yourself to a prospective employer when applying for a job. This sample shows the kind of information you should generally include.

fringe benefits the company offers (health insurance, profitsharing or pension plans, company cafeteria, or parking lot, for example). If the interviewer wants you to take the job, he, or she, may very well tell you all these pertinent details without being asked. But sometimes you yourself need to draw the interviewer out on these subjects. Learning to do so, gently and deftly, may take a bit of practice, but it's well worth taking the trouble to become skillful at your own kind of interviewing. After all, it's you who is ultimately going to lose or profit from an association with this prospective employer.

Try to squeeze in as many interviews as possible. Don't take the first job that's offered, unless it's overpoweringly attractive. Be discriminating and, when you do make your choice and start working, be professional and committed. However, if for any reason the job turns out to be definitely not your cup of tea, don't hesitate to begin looking for another. It's not necessary to quit while you search for something better. You can look while you work, fitting in interviews on your lunch hours. The important thing is to make certain you get out before you get stale. Ask any woman who has spent years in a dreary, dead end job before she forced herself to find something with more challenge and potential. Without question, she'll tell you she only wishes she'd done it sooner. Remember, if you do find it necessary to begin job hunting again, this time around you'll be far more certain about what you want, and far more confident in your ability to get it.

Thus far, we've been talking primarily about full-time jobs. But what about part-time, temporary, or at-home work? All three are fine for the woman who has a bit of time on her hands, and is well enough off to investigate possibilities other than full-time employment. But for the woman who really needs money, all three have severe financial

RESUME

Harriet L. Meyer
117 Bolton Avenue
Rochester, New York 13712
Phone: 540-7172

September 25, 1972

Job Objective   A position in the field of personnel administration or public relations.

Job Experience 1967-72: Part-time interviewer (three days per week) at the Lois Feldman Employment Agency. Specialized in finding jobs for working mothers. Responsible for initiating and coordinating contacts with new businesses for the agency.

1965-67: Assisted in setting up local newspaper (The Rochester Weekly). Helped establish format, wrote lead articles, solicited advertising copy.

1960-65: Volunteer work. Served on committee to establish community nursery school. Worked two days per week as teacher and assistant administrator.

1957-60: Assistant to Advertising Manager, Kittenger Manufacturing Company. Responsible for writing copy for annual 20-page catalog. Arranged and supervised promotion schedules. Prepared monthly reports for company director. Left to have first child.

1955-57: Secretary to Personnel Director, Bryce and Fenton Department Store. Arranged interviews and handled correspondence, as well as doing general secretarial work. Promoted to Advertising Department. Wrote copy for seasonal catalogs.

Education   1951-55: State University of New York at Buffalo. B.A. in English literature; sociology minor. Advertising Manager, college yearbook. Served on staff of weekly college newspaper and Student Council.

Personal   Born: July 31, 1934.
Marital Status: Widow, two children ages 11 and 12.
Health: Excellent.

Special Skills Experienced interviewer; able to express self well in speaking and writing; good at working with people and facilitating useful contacts between them; able both to assume and to delegate responsibility.

References on request.

drawbacks. Even despite the apparent benefits for the woman with young children, who wants to be there when they need her, the financial equation between advantages and disadvantages doesn't work out in her favor. Just a few of the drawbacks are the low pay and high taxation scales; the lack of provision for paid vacations and sick leave; and the probability that raises, promotions, and fringe benefits will not be forthcoming. All of these things are particularly true when you work in your own home. At-home work for pin money is often just that, unless you work hours as long as you would at an outside job. If you're working that hard at home, you won't have time to look after the children, and get through the housework, any more than you would if you went out to work.

For the woman without children, and with sufficient income from other sources, however, part-time, temporary, or at-home work can fill the bill satisfactorily. There are all kinds of things you can do: social work, for example, or marketing research, fund-raising or publicity, library, laboratory, or office work. Indeed, a great many of the jobs mentioned earlier in connection with full-time employment can be done on a part-time, temporary, or at-home basis as well.

Finally, what about volunteer work? This is another option for the woman who wants to be active and involved, and whose first priority is not money. But again, it must be thought about carefully. It can be extremely satisfying. But it can also take up far more time and energy than you ever thought it would; involve you in committments that, for all your good intentions, you find pointless or frustrating; and, last but not least, give you a funny feeling that you're being taken advantage of. So it must be approached with as much careful consideration and self-esteem as a paying job. It helps to know what you're really interested in, and really prepared to commit yourself to, rather than simply showing up and saying, "What can I do to help?" It also helps to know something about the problem you're lending a hand in solving, and to make sure that the committee or project that's working on it has concrete aims in view. But certainly volunteer work can be a rich and rewarding experience, particularly in this day and age when so many social and community problems need solving. How about ecology, race relations, or women's equality, for example? Or the need for intelligent committed people who will help organize tenants' associations, outings for handicapped children, or visits to lonely elderly prople? Giving what you can to any of these projects can enlarge your horizons, and involve you as an active citizen of the world at large.

So there you have it: the challenge and rewards that can be found in all kinds of jobs. It's up to you to choose the one that best meets your individual needs.

Above left: this woman turned her hobby of crocheting into a profitable small business she could run from home, even with young children around.

Above: skilled typists are always in demand, and typing for profit can easily be done in your home.

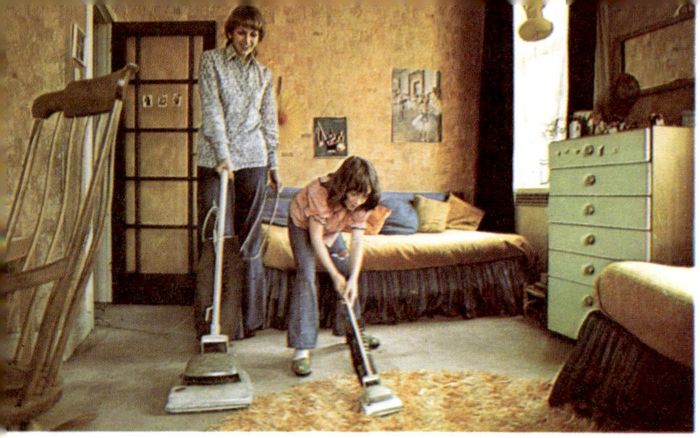
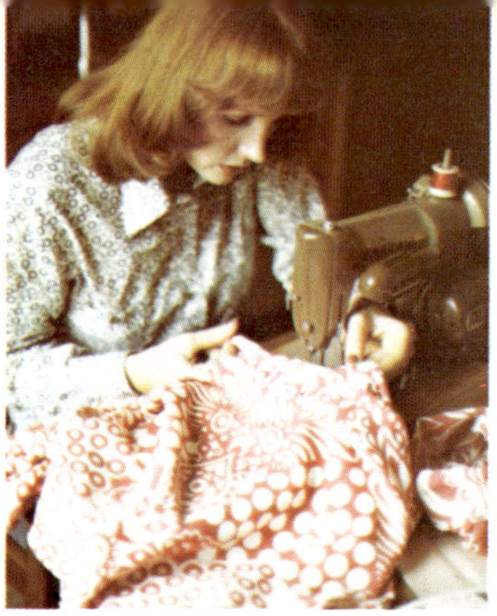
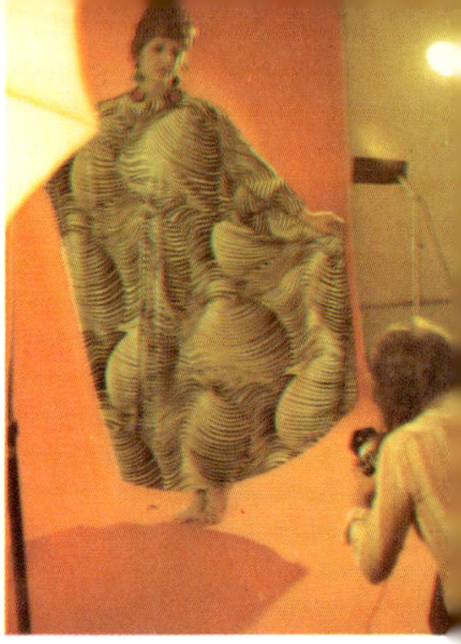
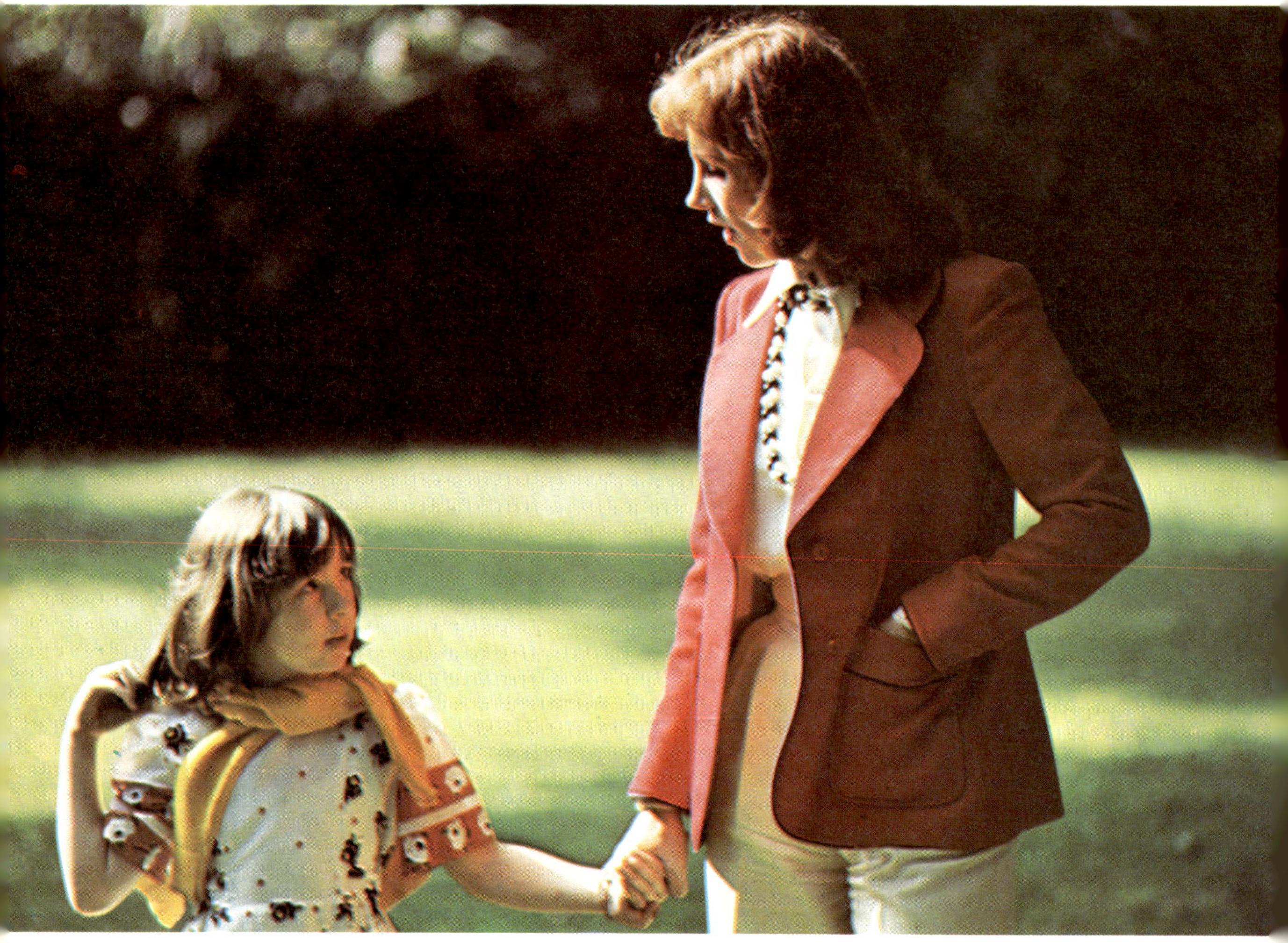
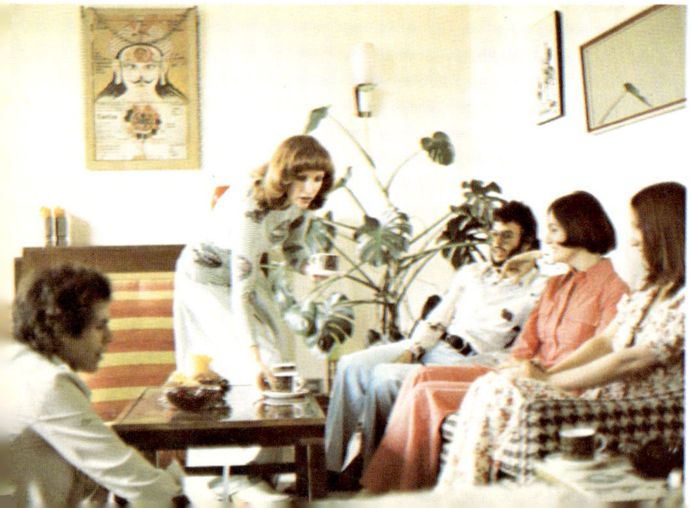
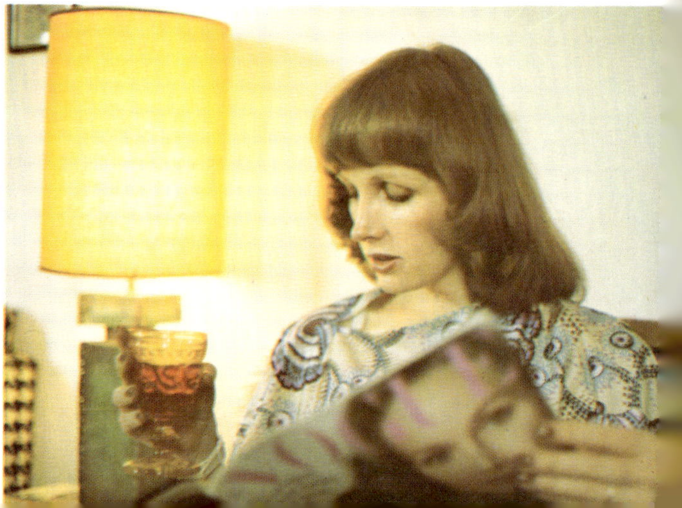

Juggling Two Roles
4

Single. Working. Mother. Just three little words, but put them together and you practically have a definition of Wonder Woman—complete with that amazing lady's nerves of steel, will of iron, and heart of gold. "Who, me?" protests the woman who is already single, working, and a mother. "I don't possess those qualities. I only wish I did!" But if you are already managing the twin roles of single parent and working woman, you already do possess them to a high degree. For there's nothing like leading this kind of double life to bring out all a woman's strength and ingenuity, resourcefulness and maternal concern.

The single working mother usually has three distinct problems to solve. First: what day care arrangements to make for the kids while she's out working. Second: how to get through the inevitable mountain of household chores without running herself ragged. Third: how to deal with that special set of anxieties that go with being only a part-time mother.

Let's take the last one first. For, however necessary her job, and however good the day care she has found for her children, a mother can lie awake nights worrying about their happiness. Without a full-time mom, won't they grow up emotionally deprived, even disturbed? The answer, thankfully, is a resounding "no." Sociologist Viola Klein, who has been studying working mothers and their children for over 10 years, puts it this way:

"If the gist of some 25 separate studies may be briefly summed up in a sentence, it is that maternal employment *as such* appears to be of no importance in the lives of children. Personality characteristics of the mother, the

There's less glamour in a model's life than we think, but it is the kind of job that allows a single mother to juggle her time more easily. For example, this young model can arrange her day around a photographic session. This way she may fit in chores, figure-trimming exercise, a good deal of time with her 6-year-old daughter—and often some socializing and quiet reading, too.

59

nature of substitute care, social class, urban-rural differences, and such factors as whether or not a mother enjoys her work, are each statistically more significant than the simple dichotomy, working—not working."

Each of us knows, deep down, that it's the quality of a mother's relationship with her children, rather than the sheer number of hours she spends with them, that really counts. If you doubt it, ask yourself what your own happiest memories of your mother are. The way she put you to bed with a special song or story, perhaps. The way she gave you her full attention when you had something to tell or confide. Her proud face looking up at you when you gave your first speech at school, or took part in the Christmas play. The times she helped you make valentines, or worked with you over some particularly difficult homework assignment. The evenings you both sneaked away from the kitchen to watch something special on TV, or the Saturday mornings when you went off together to fight the good fight at the supermarket. It's moments like these that matter to a child, and moments like these that you—just like any other mother—can share with your children.

Every working mother is subject to one or two special temptations where her children are concerned. The first is to be too lax with them over matters of discipline, as a way of making up for not being there full-time. But discipline can be a way of expressing love too, and every child needs to know that his mother cares enough about him not to let him get away with murder. Though it may seem a bit hard to insist on certain standards of behavior when you get home at night, everyone—you included—will benefit in the long run.

Discipline is the key to another temptation common to working mothers, only this time it's self-discipline. It's all too easy to spend half your time at work worrying about the kids, or phoning to make sure they're all right. A daily phone call when they get home from school, say, is fine. But constant preoccupation with their welfare will do nothing for your performance at work, and, on the other hand, the kids will get along better without frequent reminders that you are not at home.

It's just as easy to allow a certain green-eyed monster to rear its ugly head where the kids' mother substitute is concerned. Are they coming to love her too much—even, oh horrors, to slip up from time to time and call

Women who tend to children for others—usually those who can afford it—have a venerable history. Left: this Roman nursemaid is part of a detail from a bas-relief sculpture on an ancient sarcophagus. Below left: the Nanny of Victorian days often had a large brood of boys and girls under her charge. Below: the Nanny, dressed in uniform in the traditional way, is still found today in modern England.

her "mommy"? If they do love her, be grateful, and steel yourself not to feel jealous. Learning to love more than one person, especially when a child has only one parent, is in fact good for him. Don't worry, either, about his coming to depend too much on the other woman in his life. You and you alone are his mother; you and you alone will remain his mother whatever happens. As long as you yourself don't abdicate that role—in terms of your own love and concern for him—the distinction between the permanent and temporary people in his life will be reassuringly clear. Incidentally, if it happens that one beloved mother substitute has to be replaced by another, the unchanging nature of the real mother-and-child relationship will act as a safeguard against hurt and worry.

In Sweden they call her a "day mother"—and that is very much what she is. For the woman you hire to look after your children while you go out to work is a substitute mother. A good one is a treasure.

So how about that mother substitute? Clearly, finding a reliable, motherly person who can work full time is a vital necessity for the working woman with children under three. Infants and toddlers simply don't thrive under group care; they need as much of a one-to-one relationship as they can get.

A part-time mother substitute, or motherly housekeeper, is also necessary for the child in kindergarten, grade school, or junior high. However grownup he may seem, it's simply not fair to expect a child under 15 to look after himself until mom gets home. "Latch-key" children have a sad way of becoming social casualties. Occasionally, of course, it's possible to arrange for your child to attend some community or church after-school program. But in most cases, such facilities are either not available, or fail to provide the kind of individual attention a youngster needs. Whether his school day ends at noon or at 3:30, he needs someone who cares about him to come home to. This is just as true whether the home is his own, or that of a relative, neighbor, or understanding friend of yours with children his age.

Locating the right mother substitute for your youngsters can take time and patience—unless you're one of those lucky souls with a mother, mother-in-law, sister, or close friend who is willing and able to become your stand-in on a regular basis. If this kind of ideal solution doesn't present itself, however, you have to start looking. Where? Your own neighborhood may be the best place to begin. Perhaps that pleasant and capable woman upstairs, across the street, or down the block, whose own children are now at school, might be interested in looking after yours, and earning a bit of extra cash at the same time.

You could also inquire about part-time or full-time help at community clubs for older people. What about having an older woman look after your children? Don't dismiss the idea out of hand. Many an older woman is as vigorous in body, and as flexible in spirit, as women half her age—and many an older woman positively thrives on caring for children. She may even have more patience and ingenuity with small children than you yourself do.

If neither of these avenues appeals, or is open, to you, domestic service agencies, baby sitter agencies, and classified ads can be a good place to look. Local churches and child welfare agencies may also be able to offer some suggestions. If you only need part-time help, there are still other places to try—hospital placement services for student nurses, for example, or the placement offices of local high schools and colleges. Where students are concerned, by the way, don't overlook the possibility of employing a young man. If one is sent your way, and you are sure that he is reliable and good with children, give him a try. Not the least of his virtues—especially if your kids are boys—would be the simple fact that he is a man, and could exert a masculine influence on them. What a relief, too, to have someone around to do all the roughhousing you don't feel up to.

Finally, give a thought to the possibility of joining forces with another single mother. If the idea of sharing your home with another woman makes you shudder, forget it. But more and more people are giving it a try. One

A suitable day care center is vital to the working mother without a family to help. You need to find one in which your child gets caring, individual attention, and which also has a variety of activities.

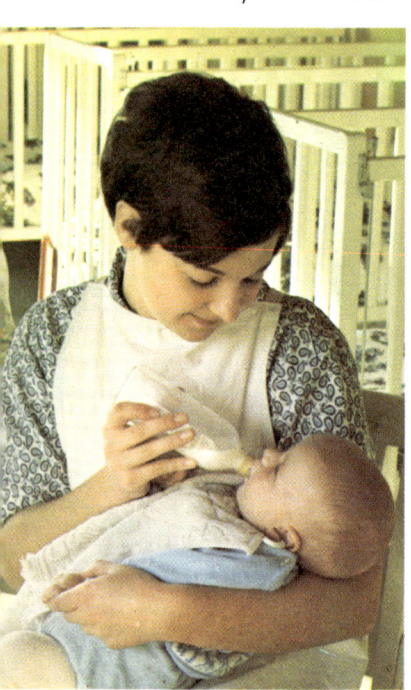

of you works, the other stays at home to look after the kids. It's surprising how well this can work, because some women really want to have a job, while others really want to devote themselves to child rearing.

Whether you're looking for part-time or full-time help, once you've lined up a few prospects you come to the difficult business of interviewing them. How on earth can you tell whether this or that person is suitable? Sometimes, regrettably, a promising person has to be ruled out right away because you can't pay the salary she needs, or because she can only stay until 4:30, but you get home at 6:00, or because she can't promise to work for you longer than a few months.

Supposing it's "all systems go" where such basics are concerned. How do you know if she's the right one? Two things should help you make up your mind. First, how does she relate to the children? If she's right for your kids, you'll know it in the way she talks and listens to them. Does she greet them naturally and easily, for instance, or go all gushy and tell them how absolutely adorable they are? Does she sense immediately how shy Jenny is, how much Doug's collection of toy trucks means to him?

Second, how do you and she hit it off? Do you like her? Can you be honest with her? Do you understand each other? Do you get the feeling, after discussing her previous experience with children, and the particular needs and problems of your own, that she'd handle certain situations as you would? This is vital, for, although no one is going to react to, deal with, cuddle, and discipline the kids just like you, there shouldn't be any major and confusing differences in your basic approaches.

Once you've made your choice, and she's begun working for you, give her all the support you can. Try to be with her for the first few days to help her get the hang of the children's daily routine, and the way you do things. Be prepared to keep your priorities straight. If, for example, she turns out to be no whiz at housekeeping, but marvelous at drawing Jenny out of her shell and handling Doug's occasional tantrums, you've got a

65

Above and right: music and the first steps toward reading—these are some of the mind-stretching things that are also fun for tots in nursery school.

winner—even if the house is a mess. If, however, you sense that the children's comfort and happiness is going to come a poor second to her ideas of good behavior and orderliness, waste no time in replacing her with someone whose priorities are more like yours.

Thus far, we've been talking about full-time and part-time care for toddlers and grade-schoolers only. What about a child who's over three, but under school age? Perhaps you feel it's time he spread his wings a little, and spent more time with children his own age. Perhaps he's your only child, or the only child in the family for whom special arrangements need to be made. Ideally, what you'd like for him is the kind of day-care center at which you could drop him off on your way to work, and pick him up on your way home. Where do you find one?

Despite the hue and cry for more child-care facilities of this kind, there aren't nearly enough of them as yet. Nonetheless, many do exist, in the form of day-care centers and nursery schools, play groups and play schools. Some are privately run. Some operate on a cooperative basis, with parents pitching in to

Above: now they're in school proper, and you know they are all right during school hours. But the single parent still has to arrange for some afterschool care if she's holding a regular job.

do whatever they can. A working mother might be asked to help with fund-raising or clerical work, or to provide a stand-in helper at the center one day a week. Some nursery schools are organized by churches, voluntary social service agencies, or community centers. Still others are run by local government agencies, or are connected to public schools, local colleges, and universities.

All of these are avenues to try. If, even after inquiring at local churches and community services, and buttonholing all your friends and neighbors, you still come up with a blank, visit a family social service agency. It's their job to know what kind of day-care centers are available near you.

However many—or few—day-care centers you come up with, the watchword is: select, don't settle for. Visit them, ask questions, and keep your eyes open. Some operate for the full working day, others only part of the day; some are open year-round, others only during school term. But whether part-time or full-time, the really good ones give the kids lots of individual attention, a well-rounded schedule of activities, plenty of indoor and outdoor space to run around in, and a wide variety of sturdy play and learning equipment.

The quality and quantity of the teachers is

67

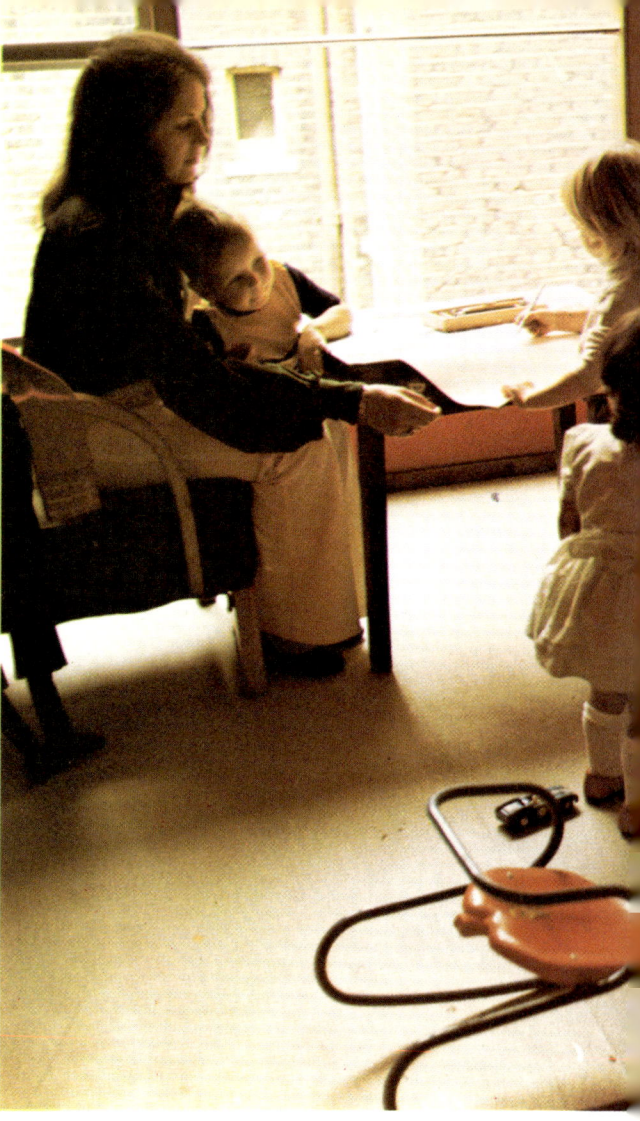

crucial, of course. There should be no more than 10 children per adult, and at least one of the people in charge should be certified for nursery school teaching. Both teachers and assistants should be the kind of people who not only like, but respect, children. Are they warm and cheerful, patient and responsive? How do they handle special problems—like the classroom bully, the timid loner, or the child who isn't completely toilet trained? Are the teachers available for conferences with the parents occasionally?

There are other points you'll want to check on, too. Does the building meet with local fire, safety, and health safeguards? Is there a nurse on the staff, or a doctor on call? Is the outdoor play area fenced in? What kind of snacks and/or lunches do the children get? Are there transportation facilities available if you cannot ferry the child to and from the center yourself?

What about the fees? These can range from a few dollars a week at centers run by public agencies, community centers, churches, and cooperatives, to as much as $1000 a year at privately run nursery schools or play groups. In some cases, scholarships or sliding fees based on ability to pay are available.

When you've found a center you like, it's a good idea to attend it with your child full-time the first day, and part-time the next day or two. Most children adjust amazingly quickly, but it helps a lot if you can be there for reassurance at first. It also helps if you refrain from being encouraging. Let him sit on the sidelines with you for a while. In his own good time, and without any urging from you, he'll soon be making forays into the

One English city council provides a special apartment building for single mothers, and Penny Johns—a 24-year-old separated from her husband—lives there with her two sons under three. With a supervised nursery provided at modest cost, Penny has been able to take a part-time job to augment her particularly skimpy budget. Although she was warned away from living with a group of women alone, she finds it comforting and congenial. "There's always someone to talk to here", she says. Penny is seen with her sons outside and inside the apartment.

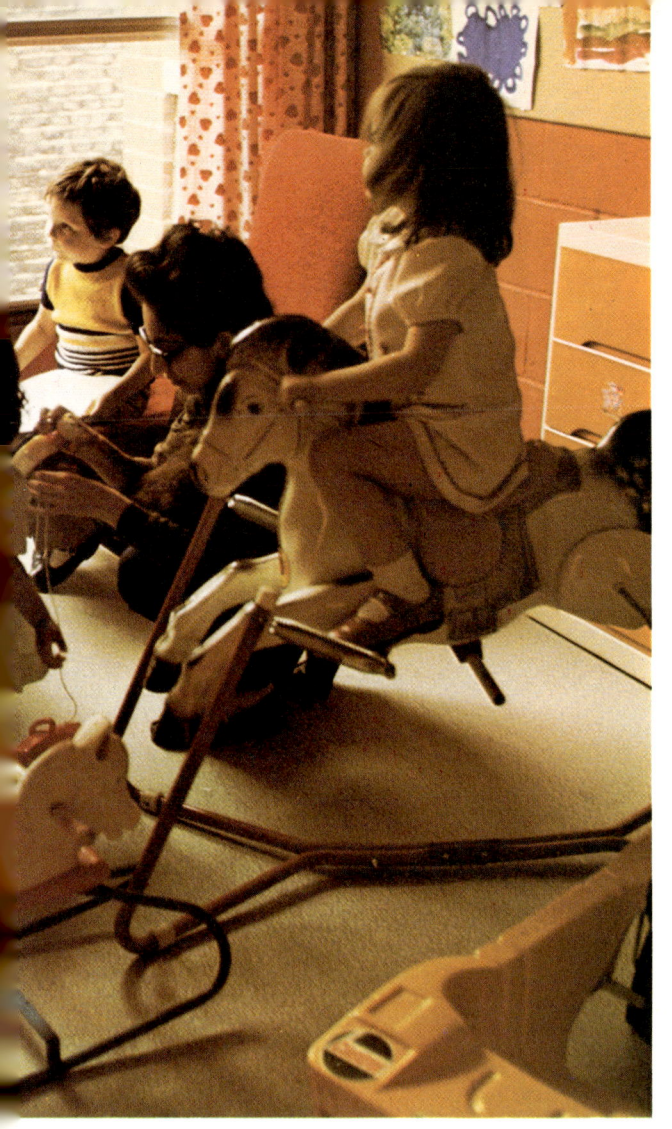

center of things, and finding that joining in is a lot more fun than just watching.

Whether a child is in a day-care center, or attending school, there is one recurring hassle that you have to be prepared for: what to do when he gets sick. Should you or shouldn't you stay home from work to nurse him? If he's seriously ill, of course you must stay home, making proper arrangement at work to do so. If, however, he only has a simple cold and a slight temperature, you'll often have to make the decision to go off to work as usual, leaving him in the care of someone else. But who? If you have a part-time mother substitute, the problem is usually solved. If you don't, however, you'd better make sure you have at least one person you can call upon as an emergency stand-in. Lining up reserve helpers, be they relatives, friends, or neighbors, before a minor crisis like this occurs can be a real sanity-saver. Then, on those days when one of the kids wakes up feeling too low to go to school, but not low enough to stay in bed, you can go into your "Battle stations!" routine, and arrange for his care with the minimum of strain.

Then there's the challenge of what to do with the children during school vacations. Arriving with clockwork regularity, they can pose a real problem, especially if you haven't thought about it in advance. Some working mothers solve it with the help of understanding relatives—married sisters or brothers, for example, or the kids' grandparents. Some divorcees whose ex-husbands have remarried arrange for the children to go to their father at vacation time. Some women find that the best solution is to employ a mother substitute for the duration. A responsible student in need of a summer job can be the answer.

Still other single mothers opt for a summer camp. If the kids are old enough—seven or eight at the very least—and you can afford it, a full-time camp can offer your kids a wonderful chance to develop new skills, and taste the joys of fresh air and freedom. If they are still too young for full-time camp, or it's just not possible financially, a good day camp can be a happy solution.

How do you go about selecting a camp for your children? Their school may be able to offer suggestions. So may some of your friends with children the same age. Another source of information is the American Camping Association (address: Bradford Woods, Martinsville, Indiana). Finally, there's an excellent booklet called *How to Choose a Camp for Your Child* by Ernest Osborn. It's obtain-

When your children are out of school for the summer, and you wonder what to do, remember that older students are also out of school, and often looking for work. Getting a responsible student to look after the kids—and take them on museum adventures and such—is a good idea. If he's male, so much the better in the way of providing a father figure.

able by writing for Pamphlet Number 231 from the Public Affairs Office, 22 East 38th Street, New York, New York, 10016. Such sources will help you pinpoint the kind of things you're looking for in the way of program and fees, administration and staff, physical surroundings and facilities, health and safety precautions.

In picking a camp for your children, you have to be as careful as you would be in picking a day-care center. You'll want to take a look at it yourself, and have an interview with the director before you decide on it. Just because it's a camp doesn't insure that it's going to be a happy and healthy home-away-from-home. It's also vital to be sure that your children are ready for camp.

Finally, we come to the biggest test of the single working mother's energy and ingenuity: housework. When you have children and a full-time job, you have to become an efficiency expert where homemaking is concerned. It's either that, or become some kind of latter-day martyr to the demands of cooking, shopping, washing, and cleaning. Priorities have to be overhauled and standards readjusted to get through it all without running yourself into the ground. The amazing thing is that it can be done, and once you get the hang of it, you'll wonder how you ever spent whole afternoons doing what it now takes you 30 minutes to accomplish.

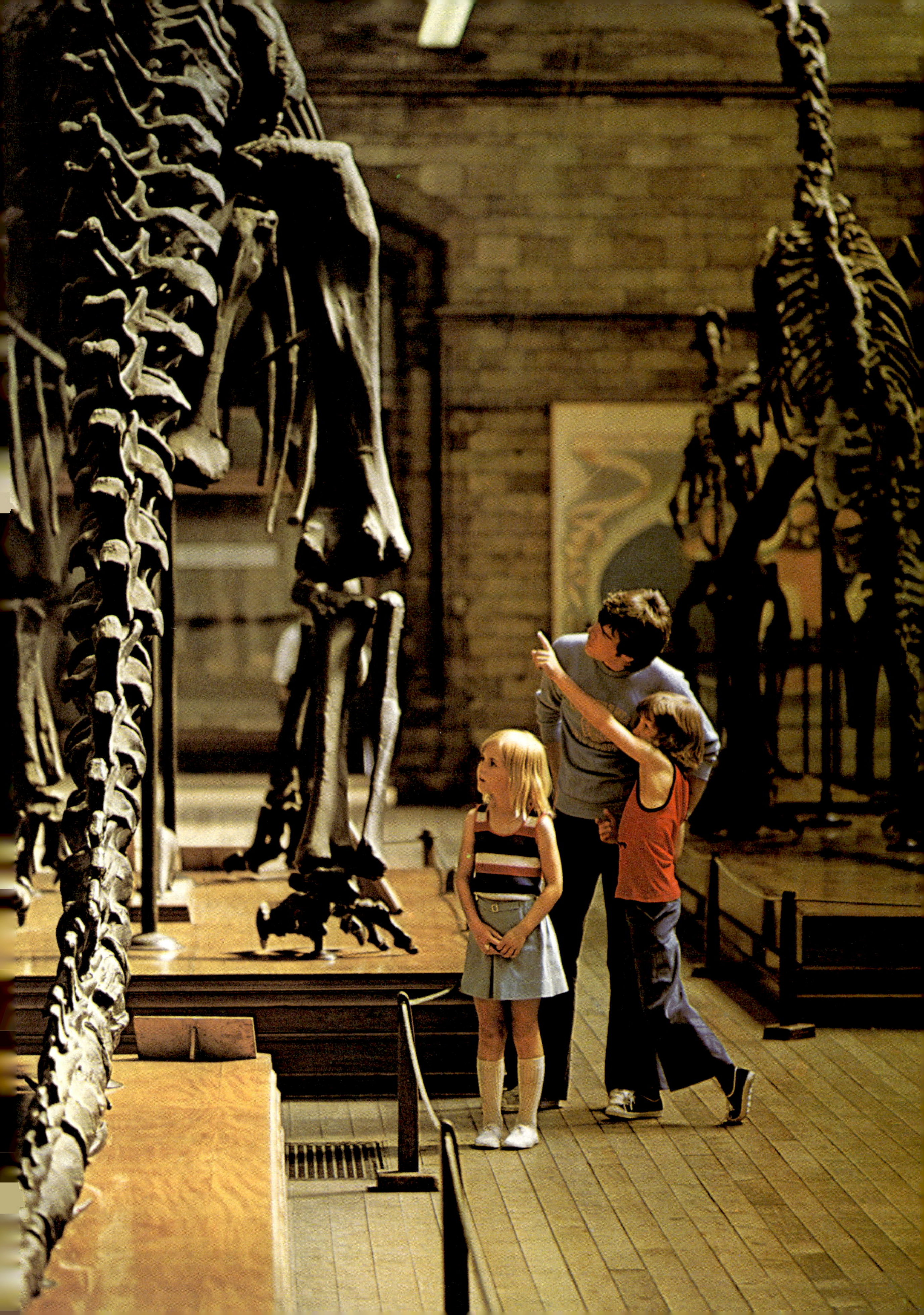

Summer camp is often the answer to a prayer for the single working parent with children at home. If your children are ready for camp—and you should be sure they are—it provides lots of healthy outdoor activities fun at mealtimes and around the campfire, and friends of their own age.

We're not going to give you the full household tips routine, because each woman has to work things out according to her own particular needs and priorities. It's no good telling you to get up early, and do half the housework before breakfast, for instance, if you're basically a night person, and prefer to do things in the evening. Of course, shopping by phone, and hiring outside help for the heavy jobs are great ideas. So is streamlining your kitchen with a freezer, a dishwasher, and every other time-saving machine and gadget on the market. But if your budget is already stretched to the breaking point, such suggestions will only make you groan. What we do propose to do is pose a few important questions for you to ask yourself, whatever your individual schedule, or financial setup.

First: Does it have to be done at all? "Do first things first, and second things not at all," has become a byword among countless thousands of working mothers. How essential are elaborate meals, gleaming windows, ironed sheets, and floors so clean you could eat off them? The answer, compared with your own health and sanity, and the happiness of your family life is—not very.

Second: Do you accept help from others? When friends or family members come over and say, "Is there anything I can do to help?" there's no reason in the world not to accept the offer gratefully. Perhaps the laundry needs folding, or Johnny's pants need a quick stitch. Maybe that stuck drawer could be fixed, or the ingredients for tonight's casserole chopped up. Believe it or not, people actually like to feel useful and needed. So if they offer, by all means accept their help.

Third: Do you think ahead? By this, we don't necessarily mean the bit about doing all the week's cooking on Saturday; many women find that cooking the evening meal while talking with the kids can be a good way to unwind after a day at the office. What we do mean is working out weekly, monthly, and quarterly shopping lists. Getting this down to a system can be difficult at first, but a real boon in the long run. You have to think of yourself as being somewhat like the homesteaders of pioneer days. Like them, you can't be running down to the store every day. What you do is get certain supplies in once a week; others, like basic staples and toiletries, once a month; and still others, like clothes for yourself and the kids, every three months. Where clothes are concerned, make sure they're wrinkle-resistant, machine-washable, and drip-dry.

It simplifies food shopping a lot if you can work out a 14, 21, or 28-day menu plan. This gives you two, three, or four basic weekly shopping lists so that you don't have to go through the whole business of figuring out what to have, and what to get each week. The result may turn out to be something like, "If it's Tuesday, it must be macaroni!" but if the meals are ones that you and the kids really like, they can be every bit as enjoyable—and twice as easy—as a new dish every night.

Fourth and finally: Do you ask your children to help? Many working mothers feel conscience-stricken about expecting their kids to lend a hand. Why? There's nothing wrong with children doing chores, provided you don't ask too much too soon. Even the littlest ones can help—by making their beds, setting the table, picking up their toys, etc. Older children can help by taking on such jobs as washing the dishes, doing the vacuuming, and putting the clothes through the wash Should children be paid for the work they do? Not, perhaps, for regular jobs like these, but certainly for the occasional bigger task like mowing the lawn, washing the windows, or cleaning the car.

Your standards have to be flexible. It helps, of course, if you take the initial time to show the children how to do chores, put things within their reach, overlook their mistakes, and appreciate their efforts. It also helps to have a regular family counsel about who does what, and how things could be simplified. You may be surprised at how ingenious the kids can be at thinking up new and better ways to do the work.

Homemaking should be a family business, especially in a one-parent home. In fact, your children may be luckier in this respect than others. In helping you, they become truly needed, and everything they contribute to making their house their home teaches them a little bit more about self-reliance, responsibility, and cooperation—as well as about what it really means to be a family.

It's almost essential for a working mother on her own to have the children help around the house—and she shouldn't worry about asking for help. Having responsibility in the household teaches self-reliance and cooperation, and makes children appreciate what a family really is. Then, after the chores—some relaxation in the fun atmosphere of a family picnic.

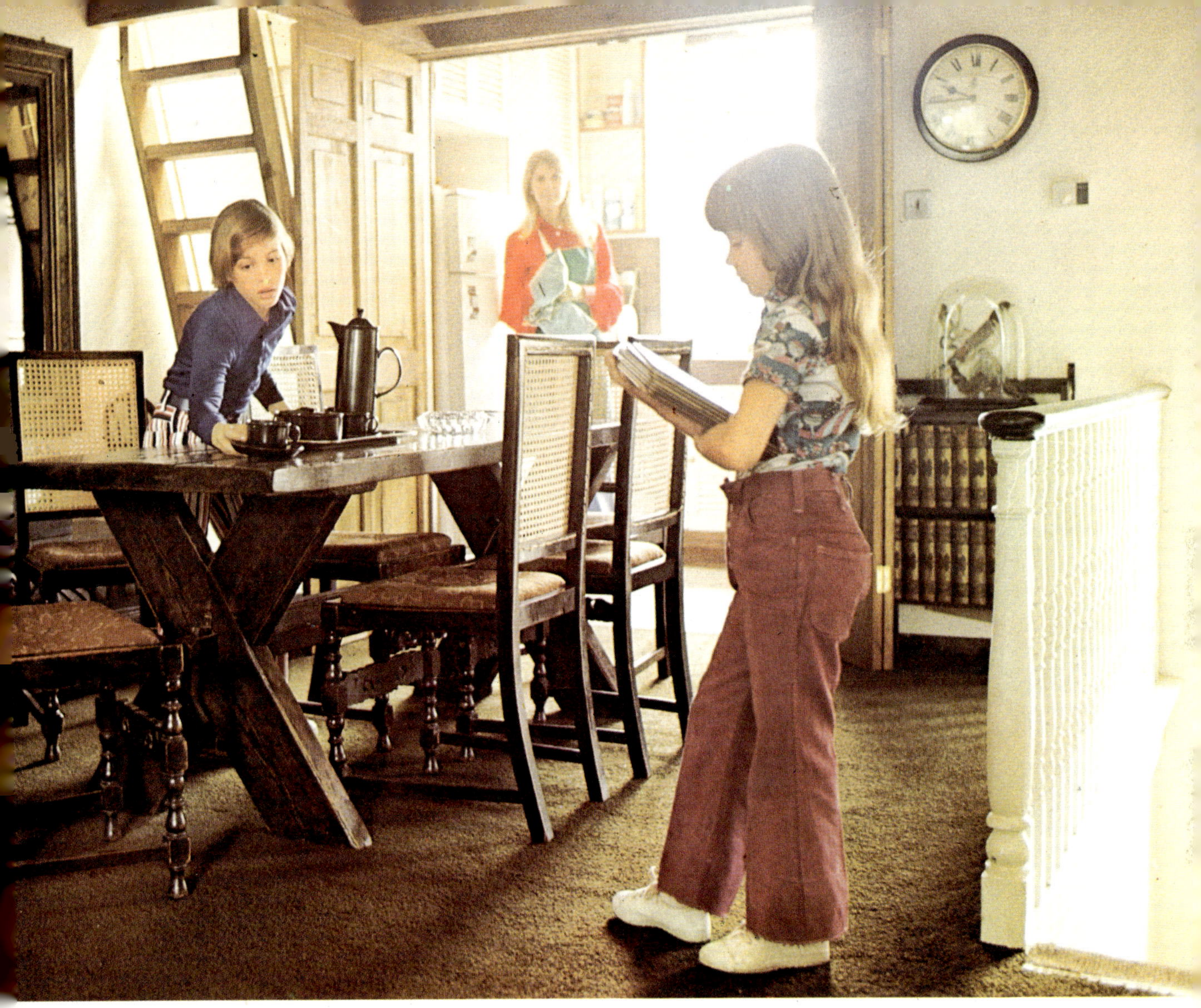

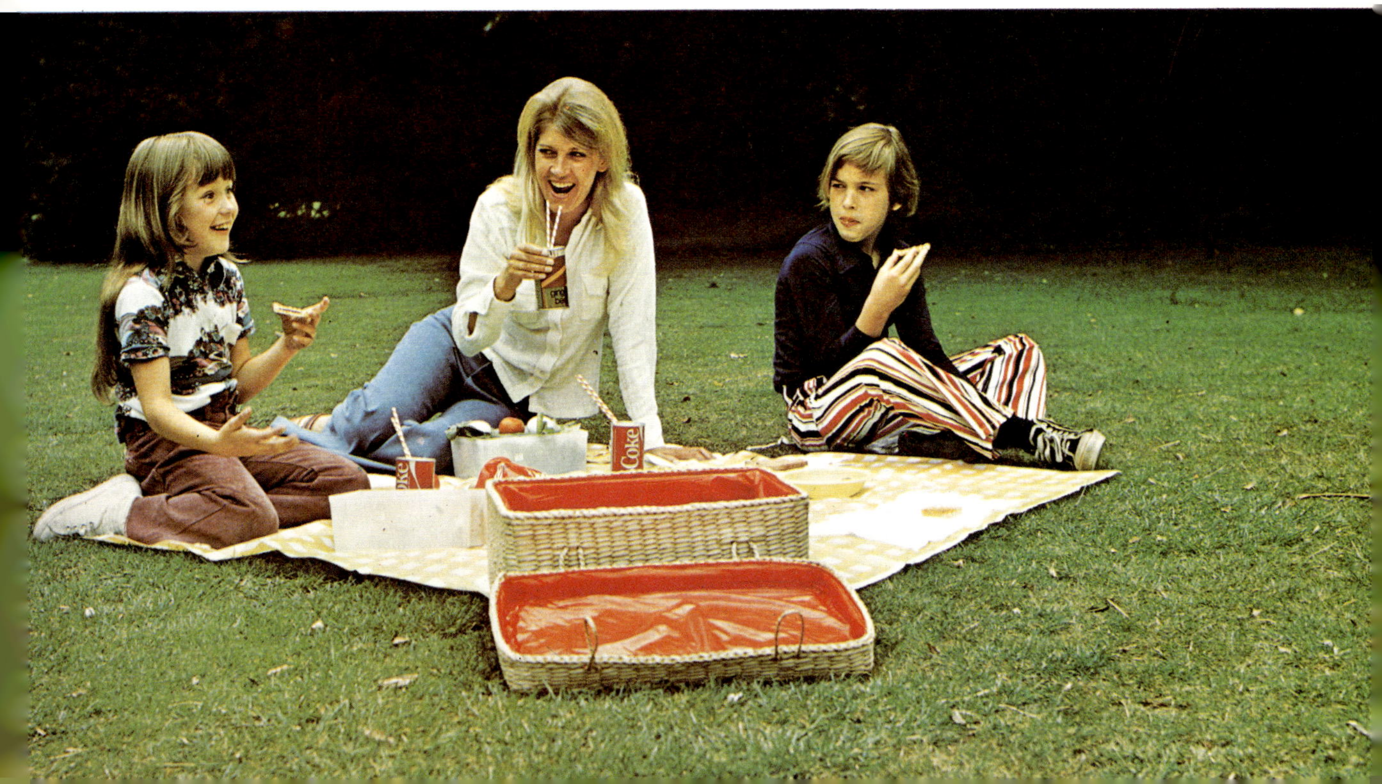
Coke
Coke

Decisions, Decisions
5

Asked what she thinks is the hardest part of being on her own, Greta Thomas, a 36-year-old divorcee, answers unhesitatingly, "Making decisions." Now Greta is not, by any means, the helpless female type. She holds down a good job, runs her home single-handedly, and is an excellent mother to her three schoolage children. But she means what she says, and her reply might well be echoed by any other single woman—with or without children to raise. For however independent and competent a woman may be, the business of making important decisions, and carrying them out, can be decidedly scary at times. Wouldn't it be nice to have someone around to consult and share the responsibility with, even to blame if things went wrong? Instead, the woman on her own finds herself faced with a multitude of choices, both major and minor, that are hers and hers alone to make—and to live with.

Without question, consciously examining your options, and accepting full responsibility for your actions, can be one of the most difficult aspects of being alone. Ours is a nation that prizes self-reliance highly, but, curiously enough, it's not a quality women are usually expected to develop. So, when a woman finds herself alone, it's natural for her to feel somewhat overwhelmed by the prospect of assuming total responsibility, not only for herself, but also in many cases, for her children as well. Indeed, solo decision-making can present a major challenge to one's confidence and courage, as anyone who's ever done it knows full well.

So how does a woman on her own come to terms with the problem? In one of two different ways, according to Patricia O'Brien,

There are so many decisions to be made, and so often, it can worry a woman on her own. But she will soon find that she can take such problems in stride—and even come to enjoy it.

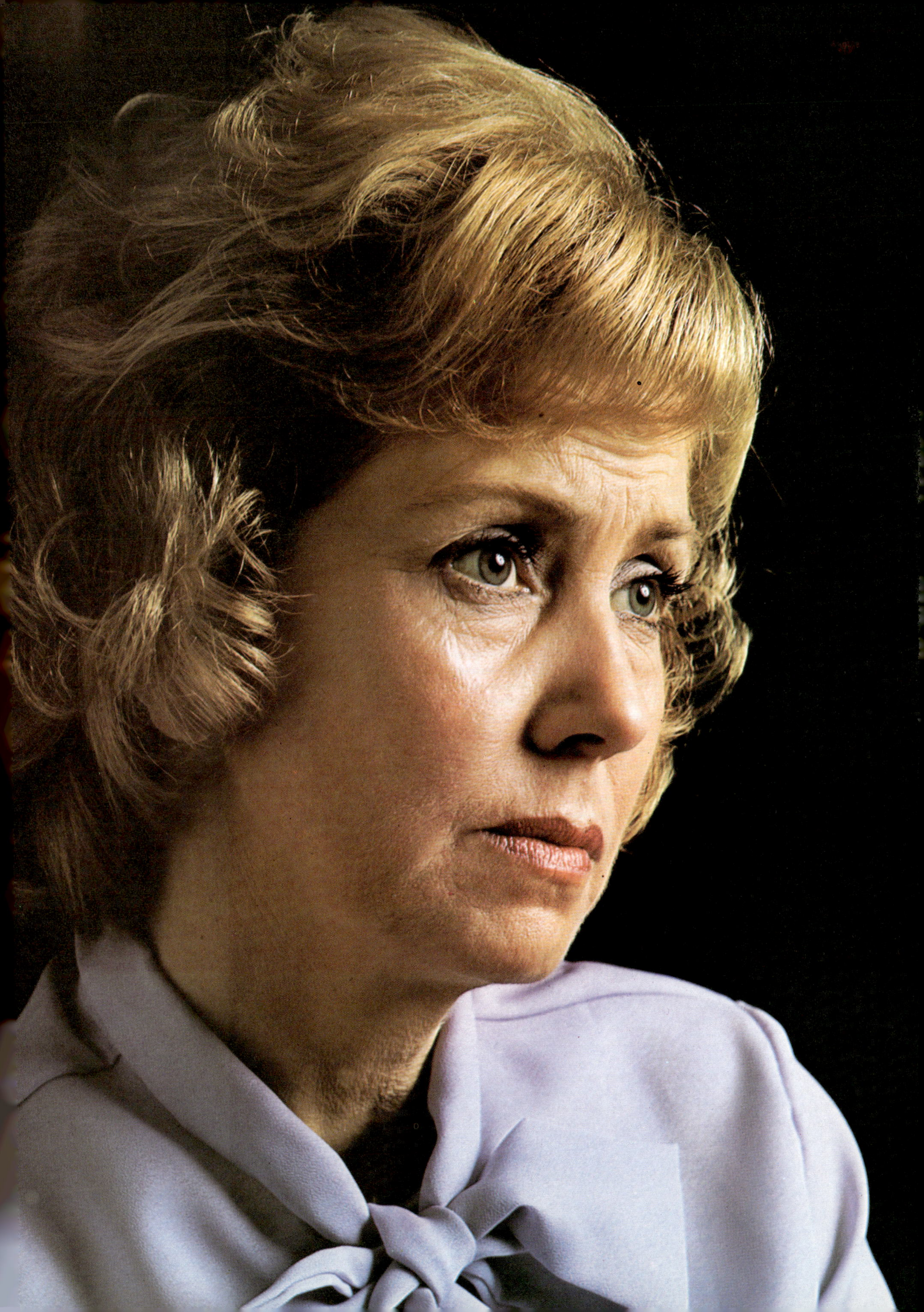

author of *The Woman Alone*. In the course of many interviews with single, divorced, and widowed women, she came to the conclusion that, where planning and decision-making are concerned, women on their own either cope, or they build. "Copers", to use her perceptive differentiation, are those who more or less drift along, taking each day as it comes, doing what they have to do, and hoping for the best. "Builders," on the other hand, leave as little as possible to sheer luck and good fortune. They use their freedom of choice to give shape, meaning, and direction to their lives, and do everything they can to make both the present and the future suit their needs and wishes.

As Patricia O'Brien points out, being a "builder" seems to have little or nothing to do with how much money a woman has, how close she is to friends and relatives, or how talented she is. It's more a question of her attitude toward herself and her life, an attitude that involves a sense of purpose and an ability to look ahead. She knows what she wants—both for herself and for her children—and she plans for it. She doesn't put off decisions concerning things like her job, the kids' education, health insurance, pension plans, and the like. She isn't just biding her time, waiting for happenstance and sheer necessity to decide her destiny. Her life, and what she does with it—both now and later—are important to her. However nice it might be for someone to come along and relieve her of some of her responsibilities, she has no intention of putting off every important decision until they do.

When it comes to giving structure and purpose to their lives, many single women

Your bank manager will often give you advice if handling the family finances gets to be a little too heavy going for you.

Right: buying a car is a major decision, so the woman on her own does well to get as much advice from others as she can before she faces the hard sell of a salesman.

without children, or whose children have grown up, positively envy those with youngsters to raise. "Why?" asks the harassed divorcee or young widow whose little brood is currently driving her crazy. For, however much she loves her kids, it's only natural for the hard-pressed single mother to feel that her decision-making would be a lot easier if she only had herself to worry about.

That's just it. Having only yourself to consider can be, in its own way, as much of a problem as having a veritable tribe to plan for. The woman who is completely on her own can be strongly tempted to put off any major decisions out of sheer inertia. Unconsciously acting on the "why bother, it's only me" principle, she can back away from making any choices, or taking any action,

Do you want, or do you already have, a home in the suburbs for your growing children? Where you live is a major decision for the woman alone—with or without a family—and it determines your whole lifestyle. It's also up to you to plan vacations, and to provide for the future education of your offspring. Ignoring things won't make them go away, so the decisions must be made. Though it may be a frightening prospect at first, you'll find that you'll grow in ability to manage as you do it.

that might really alter her life, and grow accustomed to accepting things just as they are.

It must be said too, however, that the woman with children to consider can make almost the same mistake. Faced with a thousand-and-one different tasks to get through, she may focus all her attention on today, with the idea that "tomorrow will take care of itself." Sometimes it can take a mighty effort for the single working mother to step off that treadmill for a moment, and examine the options open to her. But unless she does so, she may find that all her decisions are being made with a supreme disregard for her own future—and possibly that of her kids as well.

"It's not the things I've done that I regret, but the things I haven't done." So goes the old saying, and it's as true now as it ever was. Making plans and decisions often means taking a step in the dark, and it's doing that alone which is often hardest for the divorcee or widow who's been accustomed to relying on her husband's judgment.

Certainly, the moment when a woman realizes that all the major decisions in her life, at least for the foreseeable future, are going to have to be made by her alone can be an overwhelming one. But at the same time, it can be an exciting, even an exhilarating one. "This is it," she says to herself as she ponders some hitherto unimaginable choice. "It's up to me. Will I do the right thing?" Often, to her amazement, she not only finds that she can, but that she feels infinitely more confident for having done so. Yes, she may make mistakes from time to time, but they rarely mean the end of the world, and can usually be rectified.

She may, and most women alone do, seek the advice of friends and relatives. But if she's wise, she soon makes it a rule never to act on any advice without first understanding the reasons for following it. She's the one who's going to have to live with the consequences, after all. She may sometimes feel bewildered by the options open to her. She may find herself having to learn about all kinds of things she never thought she'd have to know—things like paying taxes and taking out insurance, making investments, and dealing with car salesmen and real estate brokers, for example.

She'll find, however, that she *can* sort out the options, and she *can* become adept at dealing with hitherto unfamiliar money and property matters. If she doubts it, she should remind herself that such things have already been made simple enough for even the dimmest man to understand. She'll find, too, that it pays to insist that things be made clear to her, even if she has to have them explained six times over. The shrewd single woman knows that she gets better results by not playing dumb, and relying solely on the wisdom and gallantry of others.

Many of the decisions a woman alone has to make boil down to nothing more than finding the most satisfactory solutions to particular problems. Some decisions, though difficult, are so inevitable that they almost make themselves. Others are so minor, or so dependent on her specific supply of time, energy, and money, that they require only a moment's thought. But there are other decisions she might want, or need to, make that don't even present themselves as decisions. Just recognizing that she does have a choice in certain matters can be a real eye-opener—and the first step toward adding zest and satisfaction to her life.

One of the most important elements in the life of any woman alone, for example, is the place she calls home. Yet it's surprising how often her home becomes a secondary consideration to her. Seeking fulfillment in the world outside, she can fail to see just how much the place she lives in is affecting both her outlook and her way of life.

To begin with, of course, there's the question of where she lives. Big cities, small towns, the country, and the suburbs all have their advantages and disadvantages. The point is, has she thought about them, and is she happy where she is? Without encouraging a mass exodus to the nation's cities, for example, it's worth noting that city life can

One of the joys of being on your own is the freedom to decorate your home in your own personal style—and part of the fun can be to make a hobby of repainting used furniture. Then, once the place looks like, or nearly like, you want it to, comes the joy of sharing its attractiveness and comfort with your friends.

have many positive fringe benefits for the woman on her own. It can cut her commuting time in half, provide her with a wide range of places she can visit and things she can do solo, and make possible a varied and interesting social life. Cities are full of single people of both sexes and all ages, who make good friends and excellent companions for spur-of-the-moment get-togethers.

It's become a truism that single women tend to gravitate to the city, but their reasons for doing so are valid. It's true that city life can be dangerous—but so, increasingly, is life in the suburbs. It's also true that city life can be very exciting. That's something that can't often be said of suburban life, particularly for the woman on her own.

There can be valid reasons for living outside the city, too. These depend as much on personal preference as on matters of convenience, security, and necessity. Small town life, for example, can provide just what one woman wants in the way of a real sense of belonging, and being known as a community member. Similarly, another woman may decide that what she wants is the peace and quiet of the country. Peace and quiet are precious commodities these days—provided, of course, that they're not all she has to live on. But if she can work out a way to make ends meet in order to live there, and also manage to keep her hand in socially, it can be an enviable way of life.

Finally, suburban living can be the right answer for the divorcee or widow with children to raise. While they are still young, she may not want to remove them from the home, the schools, and the neighborhood they're used to, and are comfortable in. Equally important may be the accessibility of her own and the children's relatives. If their father visits them regularly, for instance, his location may be a deciding factor. So may the proximity of the kids' grandparents, aunts, uncles, and cousins. Having relatives nearby who care about the kids—and their mother—can be worth every hour she has to spend commuting from city to suburbs, and back again.

Many women, after weighing up all the pros and cons of their present abode, realize that they want and need a complete change of scene. How about you? Perhaps the time has come to move to another part of the country that you've always wanted to live in, or that's nearer to people you care about. Perhaps you simply want to get rid of that white elephant of a house, and become an apartment dweller. Or maybe you just want to switch apartments in order to be closer to the center of things, or nearer to your place of work. Alternatively, you may decide that you don't want to move at all, that where you are is just where you want to be. But whether your decision is to move to a different climate, a different neighborhood, or not at all, it must be a matter of choice—your choice—based on your own particular needs and preferences.

Choice plays an even greater part when it comes to fixing up the place you call home. However large or small it may be, your home is your haven. It's also the ideal place for you to express your own special tastes, interests, and personality. Above all, it should be pleasing and comfortable to you. For home is not only where you hang your hat and entertain your friends; it should also be a place you really enjoy being in when you're alone.

Sometimes a woman on her own can make the mistake of seeing her home as a mere temporary resting place until she marries or remarries. In the interim, she tells herself, it doesn't matter if she lives out of a suitcase, eats out of a can, and lets her house remain as soulless as a hotel lobby. But it does matter. The time is now, and her creature comforts shouldn't be put off. Nor should the pleasures of creating her own special bailiwick. It's fun to discover your own personal style; it's also a way of adding a new and tangible dimension to your life as a person. Nothing can beat the warm glow of coming home, or bringing friends home, to a place that says nice things about the woman who lives there.

Some women, feeling less than whole after the loss of their husbands, fail to recognize the importance of asserting their own personality in a new, or even their old, home. Perhaps it's time for them to get rid of a few memory-charged items, to experiment with some half-forgotten ideas about what they like in the way of furnishings, even to use a little imaginative daring and give vent to their kookier home decorating notions.

The possibilities and variations on live-alone nest-building are practically endless. Nor do they require tons of money. If they do, they're probably more the product of the *House and Garden* folks than of your own creation. Rooms created one-by-one, with furniture and knicknacks of your own choosing—repainted, refinished, recovered, or simply arranged according to your own tastes—have a unique and homey quality that reflects you and you alone. Whether conventional or way-out, the way you decorate your home makes it your individual castle.

A woman's personal surroundings are a part of her life in which her freedom of choice and ability to think chiefly of herself can be allowed free play. The basic requirement is simply that she views herself as deserving the nicest surroundings possible. Sometimes, making a warm and cozy, interesting and special home for yourself alone can seem almost sinful. There's something about our Puritan heritage that keeps us from doing things purely for our own comfort and enjoyment. But, as many women alone have already discovered, having a pleasant place of their own to relax and entertain in not only mitigates, but positively enhances, the single life. And how can that be bad?

In this connection, there's also the little matter of how well you look after yourself if you're on your own. There is the harried working mother who doesn't give herself half the time and attention, particularly medical, that she automatically gives her children. There is the newly divorced or widowed woman who eats poorly, drinks too much, or just lets herself go on the theory that "it doesn't matter anymore." Then there is the woman who does nothing but worry about her health and her looks out of fear or boredom. But just as every woman needs a home she feels happy in, every woman needs the feeling of well-being that comes from taking the proper care of herself.

What this means, very simply, is looking after yourself with as much loving attention as you'd give a child in your care. You are, in a sense, your own parent. We all know the importance of fresh air and exercise, plenty of rest and a balanced diet, but sometimes a woman on her own can get into the habit of neglecting one or all of these things just because she doesn't have someone else to

> When you regard yourself as a whole person, you won't slip into the habit of not taking care of yourself just because you're a woman alone. Good grooming is always important, but so are proper food and exercise. Take care of yourself if you want the good looks that go with good health.

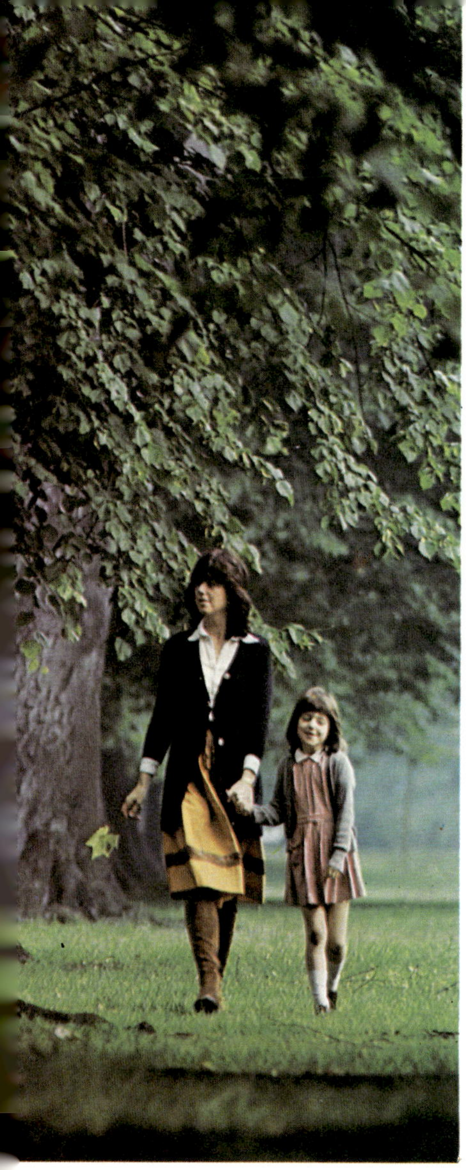
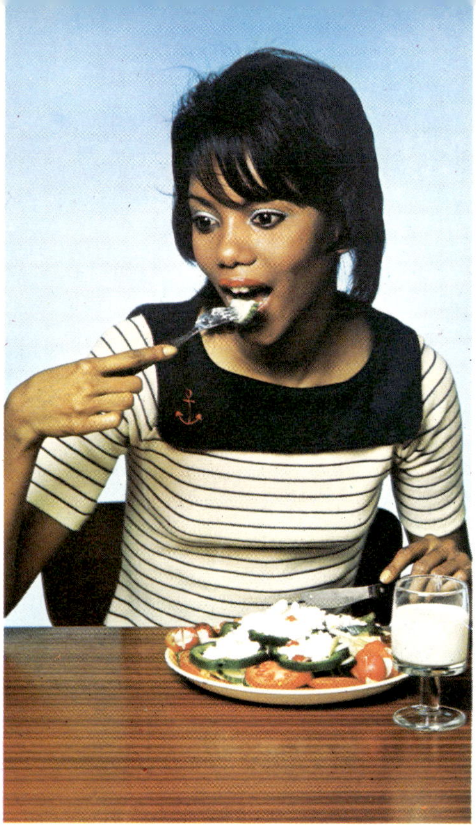
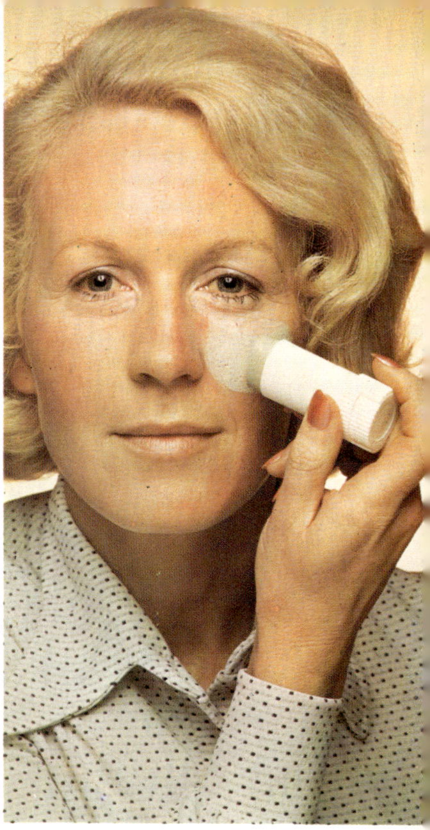
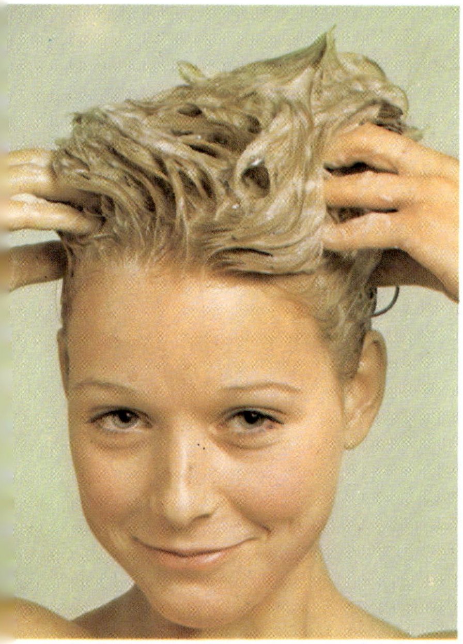
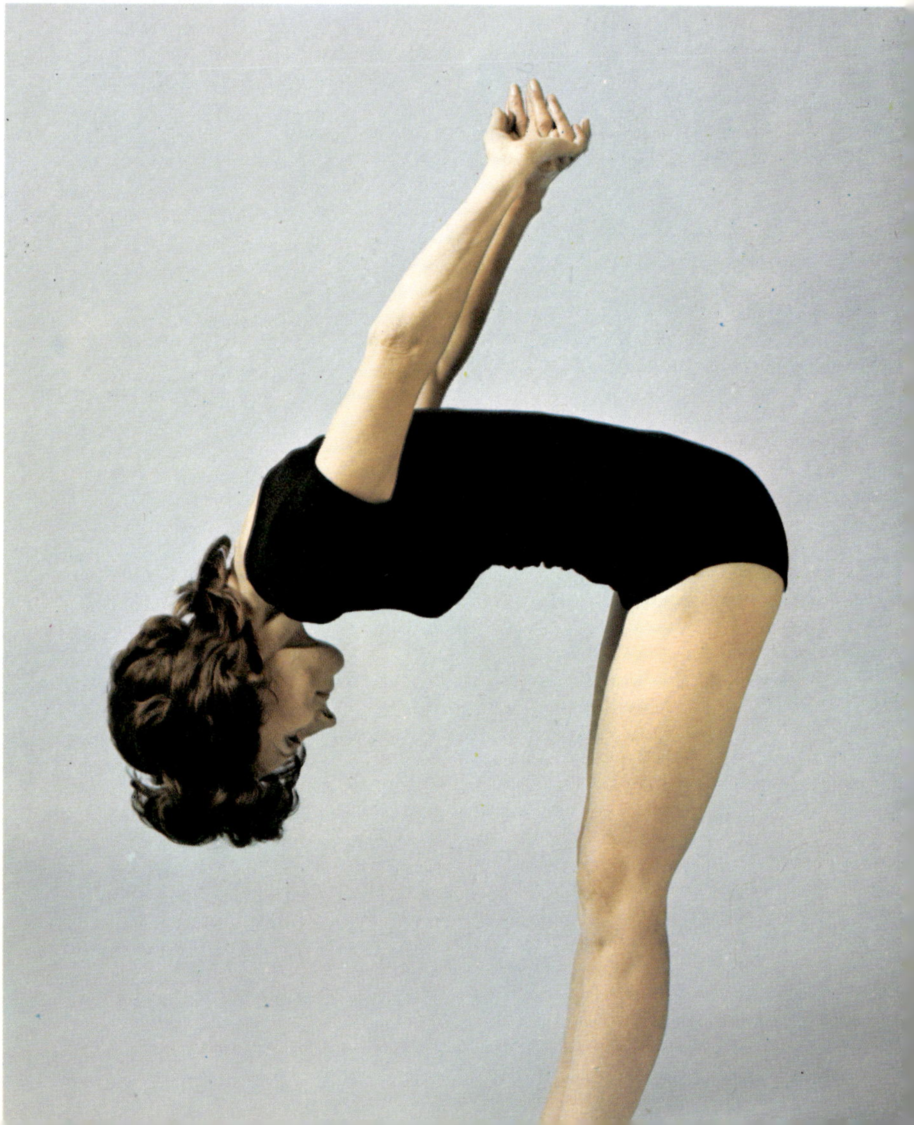

provide these things for, or to do them with.

Caring for yourself doesn't have to mean pampering yourself with all the elaborate concern of a high-fashion model. It just means giving reasonable consideration to your physical well-being. The time you spend going to the dentist, cooking good meals for yourself, and fitting in some form of enjoyable, regular exercise will pay off in every way—from health and good looks, to a more bouyant outlook on life, and a lot more self-esteem. You'll notice the difference in the way you look and feel, and so will others.

A vital adjunct to caring for yourself is, of course, guarding your physical security. Personal safety has become a prime consideration for every woman alone these days, wherever she lives. It's not being alarmist to recognize the importance of this modern fact of life; it's simple common sense. If you yourself haven't yet given a thought to this kind of thing, have a glance at the supplement at the end of this book. It includes a special section on personal security, both inside and outside the home.

A less obvious adjunct to looking after yourself is learning how to be your own handyman—that is, how to deal with all those minor, but extremely irritating, things that can go wrong with your home, your car, and your appliances. Little emergencies like these are the kind of thing women traditionally leave to a man—if not a husband or a boyfriend, a repairman or a mechanic. But there can be a lot of satisfaction in learning how to deal with them yourself. There are many excellent fixit and home repair guides for women on the market right now. There are also some good courses available on that bane of a woman's existence, car maintenance. Just knowing that you can fix things if and when they go wrong can do a lot for your morale. You don't have to spend days waiting for some expert to come and press the right button, or pull the right lever. The number of things you can do yourself, with just a modicum of know-how, will amaze you—not to mention saving you a lot of time, trouble, and money.

Choosing where to live, arranging your home to suit your individual tastes, looking after yourself and your property, taking steps to insure that your future will be what you want it to be—all these are part and parcel of building, rather than merely coping with, a life of your own. But there is another aspect of "building" that no woman alone can afford to neglect. That is giving genuine shape and structure to her daily life. Single, divorced, or widowed, with or without children to raise, working or not working, she needs to discipline her use of that precious commodity, her time.

Being on your own doesn't mean that you have to be on the go every minute, of course. Having time alone just to sit and think can be a great refresher. But doing so has to be a matter of choice, rather than a product of inertia. As most women who live alone have discovered, it's vital to make sure that your time—and your freedom—have meaning to you. Only you can give them that meaning.

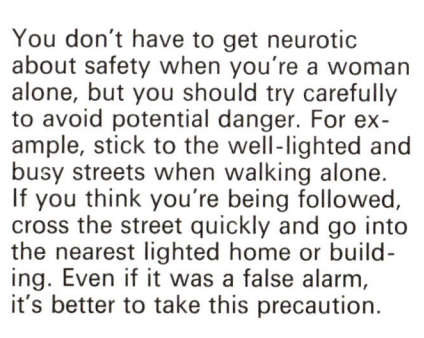

You don't have to get neurotic about safety when you're a woman alone, but you should try carefully to avoid potential danger. For example, stick to the well-lighted and busy streets when walking alone. If you think you're being followed, cross the street quickly and go into the nearest lighted home or building. Even if it was a false alarm, it's better to take this precaution.

87

Discovering who you are—and expressing that you—is one of the most rewarding aspects of living on your own. Self-reliance and independence help you to develop both your personality and your personal style.

How? By not letting the days slip by without doing those things you want to do. By exercising a little self-discipline, and organizing a routine that meets your needs and gives you pleasure as well. Above all, by careful attention to planning. Total freedom, as the woman alone probably already knows, can be as much a bane as a blessing. To get the most out of it, you have to learn how to shape it and structure it in a way that satisfies you. As one widow puts it, "If I didn't plan my days, my weekends, and my vacations with as much care as I do, I'd soon find myself just drifting along, like a ship without a rudder. I like knowing what I'm doing tomorrow, next week, even next year, and I get a kick out of being busier, much of the time, than my married friends are."

Knowing what you're doing, making decisions, and carrying out plans are all ways of discovering and expressing who you are and want to be. It's not unfeminine to think for yourself, rely on your own judgment, and plan ahead. Far from it. Nor is there anything like the satisfaction of knowing that, on your own, you can: decide to move or make a major purchase; deal with tax returns or a flat tire; take a firm line with your rebellious teenager and win through; give a dinner party or redecorate your home; arrange a special and unusual vacation for yourself or the kids; develop a personal style that pleases you; organize your daily life—and reach out for more. The more choices you make—by yourself and for yourself—the better you'll get at it. The best part of it is, that with every plan and decision you make, be it major or minor, you add to your stature as a person, and to your depth and interest as a woman.

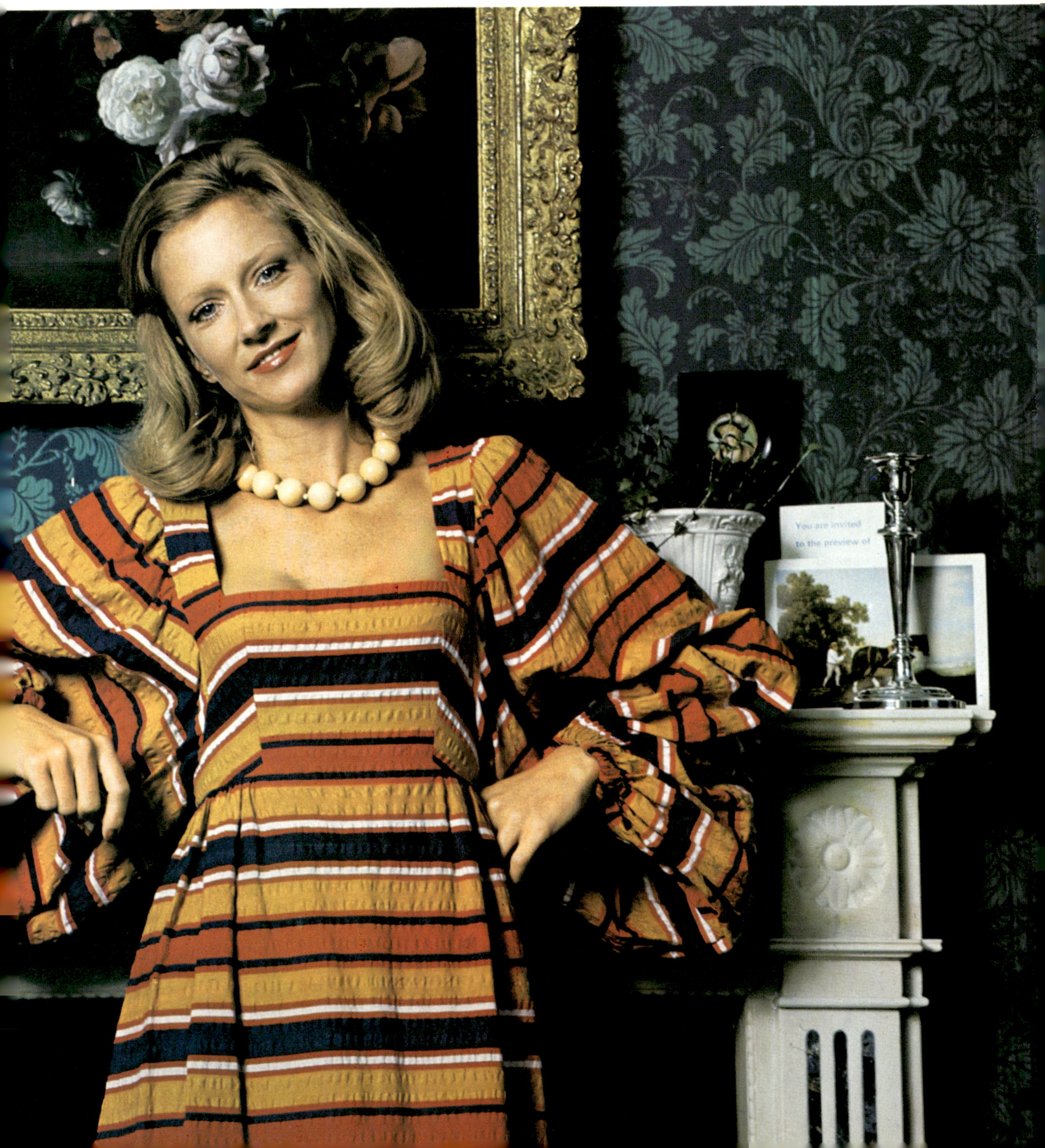
You are invited
to the preview of

Friends of Your Own

6

Above: one of the most time-honored ways of showing friendship, and entertaining at the same time, is to have people into your home for a meal. It's a good way to draw new friends, and to keep ties with old. Being a good hostess is not beyond any woman alone.

So here it is at last, you may be thinking, that word so often associated with the lives of women on their own: loneliness. Well, yes, it's a word single women themselves often use to describe a certain aching void they feel. But what do they really mean by it? When a woman says she's lonely, for example, most people just assume she's talking about an absence of love and romance in her life. Certainly the need to love and be loved by someone special plays an important part in her thoughts and feelings. (So important, in fact, that the next chapter is devoted to it.)

But there's a more generalized form of loneliness—one that, in its own way, can be even more overwhelming than the need for love. That is the need for friends. For, very often, the aching void a woman alone calls "loneliness" stems from the feeling that she's not part of the social fabric, that somehow she's slipped through the net and doesn't belong anywhere, that she has become one of life's outsiders, deprived of the kind of supportive social structure everyone else is enjoying.

This sense of social isolation can be even more painful for the widow or divorcee than for the woman who has remained single by choice or by chance. Overnight, the woman newly alone can feel herself cut off from a world of relationships she used to count on, and belong to. She needs friends now more than ever, but the old comfortable network of marriage-based friendships is no longer hers to rely on.

As this realization begins to dawn on her, the woman newly alone can feel depressed and uncertain. Here she is, single, in a world apparently made for couples. And, if she lets it, that situation in itself can make her feel that she's somehow gotten smaller all of a sudden, just like Alice in Wonderland. Without a husband, she wonders, what kind of social life is going to be possible for her?

The answer to that question is: a far more free and flexible one than a married woman usually has. For she, unlike most married women, is in a position to exercise real choice where her social life is concerned. Yes, she does face the task of making a clearing in the social jungle all by herself. But her circle of friends doesn't have to include anyone she doesn't personally like, need, and want. Every friendship she has—and she should have lots —can be an expression of her own personal tastes and interests. There's a special pleasure in making and keeping your own friends. Not the least of it is the knowledge that, because of them, you're never really alone.

At first, of course, it may be difficult for the newly divorced or widowed woman to reach out for friends. Indeed, she may begin by shrinking from any and all social contacts. Perhaps she finds excuses to avoid going out, and turns down most of the invitations that come her way. If friends ask her over, she may think, "They're just trying to be nice. They don't really want me to come." If a new neighbor asks her in for coffee, she may find some reason or other to dislike her,—or suspect

Sitting at home all alone is a good way to stay lonely. So accept that next invitation to a party, even if you think you won't like going on your own. Or throw one yourself. At some point you'll have to return the compliment to those who have invited you, so make it sooner rather than later!

her motives. "Not my type," she says to herself, "and besides, she's probably just looking for a baby sitter." If a distant friend or relative writes and says he'll be in town for a few days, she makes some excuse for being unable to see him. "I really couldn't face that," she thinks. "Maybe next time he comes . . ." Above all, she avoids situations where she'd be likely to find herself surrounded by happily married couples.

All of these defensive maneuvers are a natural and understandable reaction to the hurt of finding yourself alone. But they don't lead anywhere—except to a further sense of isolation. One of the truisms about being on your own is that things only happen when you make them possible. Head-in-the-sand tactics have a notorious way of producing no results at all. Of course, the woman alone knows this. Don't all her friends tell her so? But knowing is not always the same thing as doing. Flying solo can indeed look pretty scary to someone who's never done it before, but if a woman is not to become a hermit, she has to begin testing her wings.

So where does she start? Her first move can be a simple one: just accepting those invitations as they come along. It can be a real ego booster to discover, for example, that Pam and Brian really do enjoy seeing you on your own; that you have a lot to talk about with the girl who's just moved in next door; that Aunt Trudie from Idaho is actually fun to be with; that you can hold your own and even enjoy yourself in a roomful of couples. As you explore your potential for relating to other people as an individual—rather than merely as one half of a duo—your self-image will take on a whole new dimension. You, all by yourself, believe it or not, are interesting— perhaps even more interesting because you are by yourself.

This dawning realization makes you ready for step two: learning to be discriminating. What do we mean by that? Simply that, however self-defeating it is to turn down every invitation you receive, it can also be self-defeating to accept every one. Second only to that familiar temptation of single women

Left: the trusted woman friend who willingly offers a shoulder to lean on when needed is the subject of this painting of the Victorian period. Above: now as then, you want close women friends. Of course, there are times when you will play the confidante role in turn—but that is what friendship is partly about.

everywhere—social apathy—is the temptation to make yourself available to other people all the time, or anytime they want to see you. You have to get the old social wheels rolling, of course, before you can decide you're not going to jump on every bandwagon that passes by. But your time and your company are valuable commodities—far too valuable to be squandered. There will be pitfalls in wait for you if you simple allow the Fates, and the whims of people you know, to decide the complete pattern of your social life.

It's all too easy, for example, to form a whole raft of friendships with other women in exactly the same boat as yourself. While one or two such friends can be supportive, not to say essential, a veritable bevy of them can result in a sort of continuous "consciousness-raising session," in which you do nothing more than swap gripes and bemoan your similar predicaments. One's mental scenery never gets changed by perpetual contact with those in an identical setup.

Another pitfall is to cling for dear life to a few best friends, and ignore the rest of the world. All too often, one or the other, or even all of them, may up and move away. Where are you then? Being alone means you should have a safety net of all kinds of friendships—some warm, some cool, some ready to become warmer and more important, if necessary.

Finally, there is the temptation to become a sort of Mary Worth character. Friend to all in trouble, she welcomes everyone with a problem, and ends by having nothing but friends with a problem. Becoming a patron of strays, misfits, and those crisis-ridden people who seem to thrive on misery, can be pretty depressing sometimes. You may feel that, because of your own problems, you can understand theirs. You probably can. But you deserve more than a steady diet of other people's unhappiness. As one widow remarked after taking in a younger, suicidal friend who "needed looking after," "I've managed, somehow, to get over Pete's death, but this constant responsibility for Marianne is bringing back my blues with a vengeance."

No, you don't have to turn your back on people in need. But you do have to ask something more from the world as well: relationships with people who have a positive, healthy, ongoing outlook on life. Friendships with such people are not only fun, but supportive and happy. Every woman on her own needs contact with people who are actually enjoying their lives.

So where do you meet them? This "how to meet people" bit is something every single woman has encountered before. Yes, she knows she can take courses, join clubs, and participate in community affairs. But this advice, usually handed out like a prescription —"here it is, just fill it and everything will be dandy"—doesn't quite fit the case. Why not? Because you can't make friends the way you take medicine. Deep down we all know this, and that's why we tend to shy away from "friendship prescriptions."

Friendship, like love, is an elusive thing. It's more likely to come your way when you're not looking for it than when you are. Like love, too, it's more often a by-product of something you do than the foreordained result of your doing it. You don't take a job to make friends, for example, but you often make friends as a result of taking a job. By contrast, that art appreciation course you embark on with the sole aim of meeting interesting people can be a disappointment if you're not very interested in art, and the class is full of dullards.

The point is that any course, club, or activity you join should be meaningful to you in and for itself, rather than merely being a stepping stone to relationships with other people. This demands, of course, that you discover what it is you'd really like to know more about, or become more proficient at, or contribute to. There are classes and courses, for example, in everything from jewelery-making to film-making, French language to French cookery, medieval music to car maintenance, gestalt therapy to penal reform, creative writing to furniture refinishing, hatha yoga to glider-plane flying. There are also all kinds of clubs and organizations devoted to particular sports, hobbies, and special interests. Tennis clubs and bridge clubs, amateur dramatics groups, and professional associations fall into this category. Last but not least are the numerous volunteer and community action groups formed to push for improved living conditions for tenants, to take up arms against pollution, to provide tutoring for underprivileged children, or to lobby for or against some new law. Joining such a group can do wonders for your morale, if for no other reason than it enables you to do something about troubling current issues.

Once you've chosen something to learn, do, or take part in—something that has a real and intrinsic value to you—the meeting people part will come more naturally. Of course, it's wise to seek out the kind of class or activity that will involve talking and interrelating with other people, rather than requiring that you just sit there like a sponge, and then go home without having spoken a word to anyone. It's wise, too, to remember that everyone else is slightly shy as well.

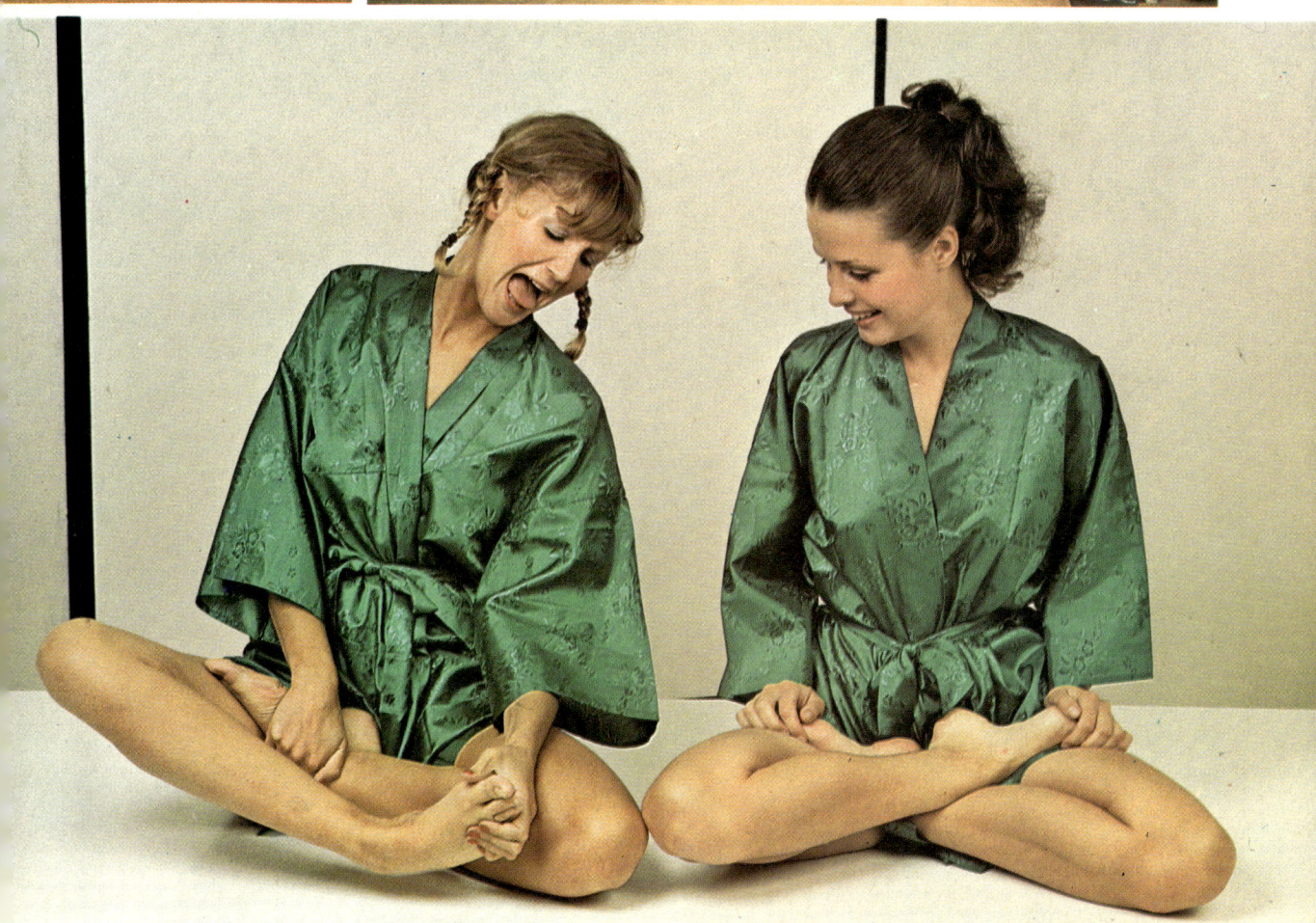

Feel in a rut? Plenty of fun things to do about it. How about taking up a help-the-figure sport, such as tennis or golf? Or, maybe you'd like to bend and twist healthily in a Yoga class. It's also good for the nerves, and a classroom is usually a fine place to meet new people. Prefer sewing? There's that, and many other hobbies of interest.

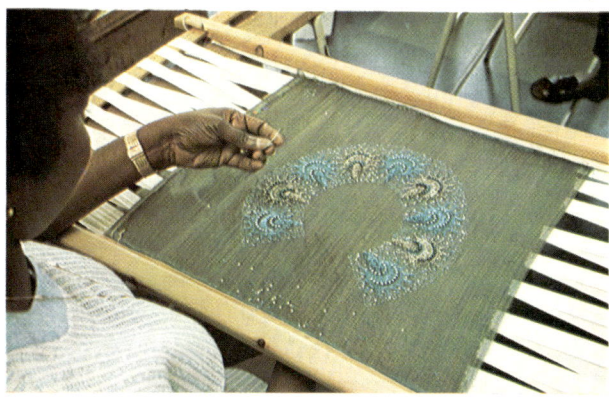

Little is going to happen in the way of getting to know people if you don't encourage yourself to speak up, and be friendly to people who interest you. Finally, bear in mind that it would be silly to throw in the towel and give up if the first class, meeting, or activity you take part in doesn't seem wildly exciting, or fails to turn up anyone you like. After all, one of the main points about this sort of thing is to learn something, broaden your horizons, and generally become more interesting to yourself—and to others. Even if the type of people you meet, or the way the class is organized, makes your blood boil, you will at least have something to chew over, talk about, and be learning from. It's all fodder for the involved and changing you, and you can't help but gain from it.

One of the most important steps in becoming your own woman, and finding your feet again socially is developing your own tastes, values, interests, and opinions. This not only makes you more of a person in your own right; it also enables you to be more flexible and more decisive where friendships are concerned. In fact, one of the great advantages of being on your own is that you can make all kinds of friendships, choosing them, or letting them go, as you alone see fit. You are not hampered by someone else's preferences and prejudices. You don't even have to worry about whether your friends get on well together.

You can, if you choose, have a mixed assortment of friendships, each of which satisfies or draws upon different aspects of your personality and interests. Indeed, it's a good idea to have as many different kinds of friends as you can. It's surprising how much you can discover about yourself—and the world—through the eyes of different people. And, like the food you eat, a balanced choice of friends makes for a healthier and happier you. What do we mean by balance? Well, simply friends of all ages, both sexes, and varying social and professional situations. In other words, older people and children, single people and married couples, co-workers and neighbors, "regulars" and "irregulars." The

Right: being on your own actually gives you more scope than most marrieds to make many different kinds of friends—male friends in particular.

Below: you can also pick and choose among all the females you meet to decide whom you want to see again—and how close you want to be.

freedom to have a few odd friends, and certainly the freedom to have friendships with men on a platonic basis, is one of the special prerogatives of single women. The idea is to please yourself in the way of friendships, as much and as often as you like.

Friendships, once again like love, can take place on all kinds of different levels, and exercise all kinds of different feelings. In one friendship, for example, you may play a chiefly giving role; in another, you may be the taker. Some friendships are formed only on a temporary basis, for short-term support or amusement. Some are on-again off-again things, enlightening, exhilarating, boring, and demanding by turns. Still others, the most precious of all, endure for a lifetime, growing and changing as you do. Friendships like these usually involve a good deal of mutual trust and consideration, a healthy respect for one another's opinions and privacy, and a lot of genuine give-and-take, whether it be in serious heart-to-hearts, or the sharing of a good laugh. Lifelong, life-line friendships of this kind are not only like love; they are love.

Every kind of friendship—from the most light-hearted to the most supportive and sustaining—thrives, of course, on care and attention. Just as a plant will wither if you just sit there and expect it to grow without light and water, so relationships tend to fade if you just sit there and wait for them to develop with no nurturing help from you. This can be one of the most difficult parts of being on your own: realizing that, as a single person, you have to make a bit more effort than you would if you were married. A couple's social life sometimes almost takes care of itself. A certain rhythm and routine of socializing gets established, and rolls on without much extra thought on the part of either husband of wife. But, in order to have a viable and ongoing social life, the single woman often has to get the ball rolling—and keep it going—through her own concerted actions. Otherwise, she may experience those awful doldrums of waiting for the telephone to ring, or facing, on Friday evening, the

Bet there's a party at your house tonight! It looks like the food will be simple but good. Maybe it's been planned for a week, or maybe you just decided on the spur of the moment to get a few friends together. This is one of the greatest freedoms you have when you're living on your own.

prospect of a dreary, do-nothing weekend.

What this involves is making plans, making phone calls, and making an effort where entertaining is concerned. If you want to keep in touch with people you care about, do so. If you want to be busy over the weekend, or over the Christmas holiday, make plans with a friend or friends before it arrives, bleak and uneventful, with everyone you know already tied up. Above all, learn the art of entertaining on your own.

This last can have a scary ring to it, and in fact is often a stumbling block to the woman alone. It's the easiest thing in the world to shrink from and procrastinate about —because you're too busy or too tired (if you have children); because it's too demanding (you think your cooking isn't good enough, you're worried about keeping everyone happy while you're in the kitchen, and who's going to fix the drinks?); or simply because you lack faith in the interest-value of your own company (who'd want to visit little old you?).

Well the very first thing to get straight is that everyone likes to be asked out, likes having the opportunity to relax and be treated like a guest, likes to feel wanted. Entertaining is a reciprocal thing, of course, and very few people continue to be asked over if they never, never return the favor. Whatever your reasons for refusing to play hostess, the end result is that friends get the impression you don't want to have them over. That can't be good for any relationship.

Another thing you need to bear in mind is how little people actually require in the way of material perfection, provided the vibes are right. In other words, entertaining is chiefly a question of good feelings. When people feel wanted and appreciated, they're amazingly unobservant about the relative shabbiness of a room, or the relative plainness of the food they're served. If you enjoy seeing them, if you get a kick out of treating them to the best you have, that in itself creates goodwill.

You don't have to entertain in a big way, either. The scale of the get-togethers you hold depends entirely on what you feel most comfortable with. It can be anything from snacks around the TV to an ambitious buffet supper, from a simple dinner party of a casserole or spaghetti and wine, to a real wing-ding of a cocktail party. The possibilities and variations on solo entertaining are many, and have nothing to do with the number of people involved, or the grandness of the food and drink you serve.

The point is simply not to be put off by the idea of entertaining alone, or by what you imagine the requirements of being a good hostess are. Every woman alone should see herself as a fully competent social animal on this score. All she really needs is the desire to please her friends, and to explore her potential as a giver. Few things are as gratifying as giving pleasure to those you like, or would like to know better. Start small, if that suits you best, and read up on easy recipes and quick-fix drinks, if you need extra bolstering. But above all, spring the lock on any preconceived notions you may have about the finer details of artful entertaining. First and foremost, entertaining others is the expression and confirmation of friendliness. Good feelings, plus a little know-how and organization, lead to good times— and the prospect of more good times. It's as simple as that.

1000
ward!
WHO CAN PROVE THAT THIS SOAP
MANUFACTURED BY
LEVER BROS.,
SUNLIGHT ON MERSEY
ANY FORM OF ADULTERATION
WHATSOEVER,
ANY INJURIOUS CHEMICALS

Loving and Being Loved
7

This may well be the first chapter you turn to, especially if you're on your own. And why not? Love is something we all need, and love, especially in connection with the single woman, seems to have an endless fascination, not just for her—that's understandable—but for everyone who knows her.

That old question, "How's your love life?" so often put to the woman alone, can be difficult to answer—painful, in fact, if she doesn't have one at present, and embarrassing if she has. If she isn't seeing anyone right now, for example, she's likely to get pity. ("You must be terribly lonely.") But if, in fact, she's enjoying a flourishing love life, she may be treated to a sort of muffled disapproval. ("When are you going to settle down and get married?")

The fact of the matter—as the woman alone knows full well—is that most of her friends and family will have fairly ambivalent attitudes about the presence or absence of love in her life. Her parents want her to be happy, of course, but happy and married. Likewise, her married friends, while secretly —or openly—envying her freedom, really wish that she'd find the right person, come in out of the cold—or the heat—and join their ranks as a regular, married woman. And her single women friends, however eager they may be to discuss their own love lives, may not be so delighted to hear about hers— especially when things are going well for her, and not for them. Unhappily, there's a certain element of competition between single women in this regard that disappears completely only when they are equally happy—or unhappy.

Whatever a woman's friends and family

Love can come at any age, and it can be just as rich and beautiful if it's for the second time. We all want and need the joy of sharing big and little moments with someone we care about—and who cares for us in turn.

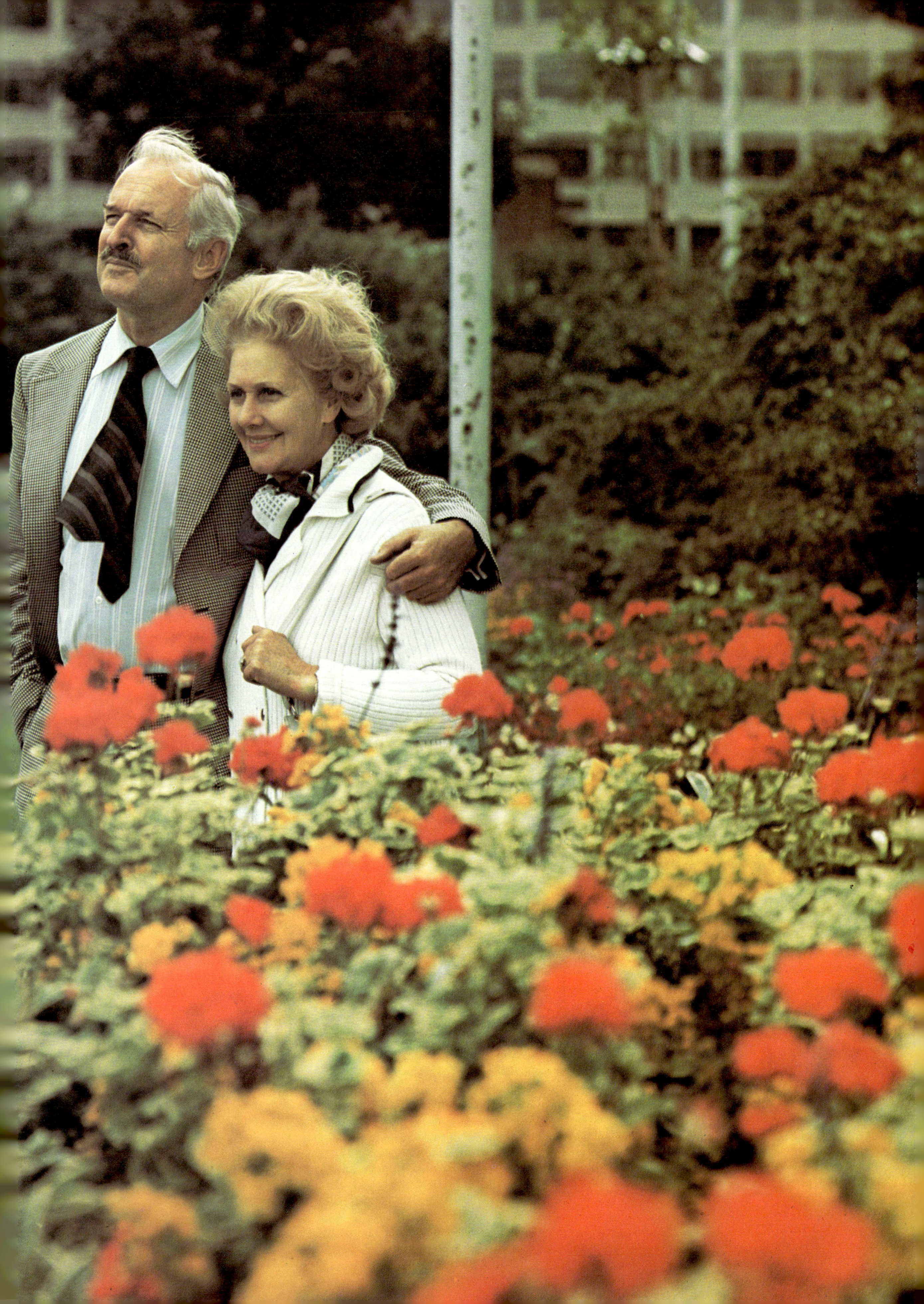

Your eyes are meeting his for the first time. Will this be romance, will he become a brotherly friend, or will the whole thing fizzle? Meetings can promise adventure for the unattached woman.

may feel about the progress of her love life, though, it's what she herself feels about it that matters most. Needless to say, it matters a great deal. For love, whether she's already found it, or is hoping to find it, is usually a continuing preoccupation for the woman alone. It doesn't matter whether she's younger or older; divorced, widowed, or as yet unmarried; with or without children; longing for marriage or content without it. Unless she's very unusual, extraordinarily self-sufficient, or too busy or bitter to contemplate it, the need for love plays a special and important part in her thoughts and feelings, all the time.

Hand-in-hand with the search for love go all manner of joys and sorrows, delights and hazards, ironies and pitfalls. It can be marvelous to be free; it can also make you wince with pain when people tell you how they envy that freedom. It can be exciting to be able to pick and choose, but supposing there's no one to pick and choose from? Women alone are vulnerable creatures, and they sometimes make mistakes. But, increasingly, they are realizing that they have as much right to love—and as great a capacity for loving—as anyone else, and that the need for love doesn't stop with age or circumstances. So right on, woman alone! The question is not whether you should love and be loved, but whom you can love and be loved by.

There are different kinds of love, of course, and different kinds of need for it. There is therapeutic love, and love-with-a-future, for example. One woman, cherishing her new-found freedom, may only want temporary relationships, a chance to feel wanted and womanly without becoming involved. Another woman may want nothing more than to cast off her independence as soon as possible, and commit herself again totally and forever.

Even the same woman may experience different needs at different stages in her experience. For a while, she may just want to be on the receiving end of attention and affection; later on, she may want even more to be a giver of them. At one point, she may long for someone to lean on and rely upon; at another, she may long for someone who needs her. At times, she may experience the need for simple companionship—someone to go out with, to share news and laughter with. At others, and on a deeper level, what she may long for is someone who really knows her, who truly understands and appreciates what she's all about, and who cares what happens to her.

Underlying all of these needs is one that a woman can feel at any stage in her experience: the longing for physical comfort and release. This can be the most disquieting need of all, for it is something she finds difficult to talk about, and yet must live with from time to time. While some might maintain that sexual fulfillment is not an absolute prerequisite for a woman's health and happiness, no one would maintain that remaining unfulfilled in this way actually adds to a woman's health and happiness. Yet it is in the search for this kind of fulfillment—a search that is sometimes for nothing more than a moment's blissful oblivion, and the comfort of being held tenderly in someone's arms—that the woman alone can feel her aloneness most acutely.

It has been said that love and sex are like scotch and water—fine together, and fine on their own. Perhaps that is true. But the act of love is not always the act of loving, and loving, of course, is what most of us want most of all. Although sex is a time-honored way of demolishing the barriers between men and women, the feeling of closeness it creates is, alas, of short duration. If there is nothing more than sex between a man and a woman, it can often make both of them feel more lonely than before.

Almost everyone has experienced this special kind of loneliness at one time or another. It's a feeling of emptiness and disenchantment like no other. Wanting so much and getting so little from an encounter like this, a woman may feel deeply distressed, almost betrayed. Living in this age of sexual freedom and experimentation, too, she may also feel somewhat surprised at herself. Here she is, free as a bird, and able to do as she pleases. So, having recognized her needs, and her right to fulfill them, why does she feel so let down? Is she being old-fashioned, and allowing her conscience to trouble her?

Well maybe so, and maybe not. For let's face it, it's often easier to express our doubts about this sort of thing in simple moral terms than in terms of something more complex: our need for love and understanding. Genuine trust and tenderness, genuine recognition and affirmation of one another as people—these are the feelings that bridge the gulf between a man and a woman, and add the final dimensions to physical love. Without such feelings, lovemaking can become an exercise in futility, a mere question of performance and mutual flattery, a way of touching without giving.

Deep down—even in this openly sexual age of ours—everyone knows this. But if a woman hasn't been in love for a long time, hasn't felt the kind of emotional warmth and tenderness that can make physical love so fulfilling, she may lose sight of all that a relationship can be. In her hunger for closeness, she may reach out for any kind of relationship, ask too little of herself and for herself, and then wonder sadly, "Is this all there is?" Of course it isn't, but it can take

He's a platonic friend—and worth his weight in gold. For having the companionship of a male with like interests, but without emotional complications, can be a great boon to the single woman.

every ounce of faith and hope she has sometimes to believe there can be more, and to turn her back on the kind of offers that basically offer her nothing at all. (Learning how to say "no", gently and gracefully, is something we'll get to in a moment.)

In the meantime, perhaps the most pressing question for the woman alone is where and how can she meet desirable, eligible, trustworthy, or just plain interesting men. For, however much she may have her heart set on finding the right man for her, she knows perfectly well that playing princess in the tower is not likely to make him come riding by. Besides, if she's like most women, liberated or not, she enjoys the company of men, and wants opportunities to meet and get to know more of them. So how does she do it?

The answer starts by being the same as it is to the question about where to meet friends. There are, for example, classes, courses, special-interest clubs, and community action groups. There are also sports activities of all kinds—swimming, skiing, tennis, bowling, golf, ice skating, etc. Last but not least, there is your place of work, and any other friendly, respectable place you're in and out of frequently—your apartment building, library, laundramat, supermarket, weekend vacation spot, etc. The advantage of all such meeting grounds is that they not only give you a context in which to size a person up, but also involve an interest or activity you have in common that you can talk about together easily and naturally.

But, where meeting men is concerned, there is also another whole social dimension full of possibilities. To begin with, there are parties, and there are your friends. What's wrong with telling people that you enjoy parties, and are interested in enlarging your circle of acquaintances? Even your best friends are not going to make any special effort if you've given them the impression you either don't need, or don't want, to meet anyone new.

When you do go to parties, enjoy them. This means not clinging to the one or two people you already know, and not playing the passive, "I'll wait till they come to me" role. At any social gathering, there are other people just as shy and just as uncertain as you are (and they're not just the creepy ones, either). They like being sought out and talked to. You don't have to be as beautiful as Mata Hari, or as witty as Dorothy Parker to make an impression on them, either. If your sense of yourself is that of a whole person, an interesting and valuable woman, with tastes and values all your own, you can't help but arouse others' interest in you. This, of course, is all the more true if you feel a genuine interest in others. Every party you go to can be secretly regarded as a kind of social experiment, a chance to test your own special chemistry as it reacts with others. You're bound to come in for a few pleasant surprises along the way.

Much the same thing applies to arranged dates with someone known to a friend or a relative, and even blind dates with someone known to a friend of a friend or relative. Naturally, such dates don't always work out, but perhaps it's unwise to shun them altogether. Even today, people do sometimes meet the right person, and fall in love, on such dates.

Yet another avenue to try if it appeals to you at all are the numerous facilities especially designed to bring single people together. There are residences, meeting places, clubs, and bars for singles only. There are organizations like Parents Without Partners, and, of course, the computer dating gambit is yours to try. Don't knock it till you've tried it; it actually works for some. Finally, there are the numerous vacation spots geared chiefly to singles. Where this last idea is concerned, bear in mind that you needn't spend a full vacation in such a setting. A few days away at a beach or ski resort is a lot less costly, and still gives you the opportunity to meet people. It is becoming an increasingly popular way for people to meet, in fact, and has the decided extra benefit of a break that does something for your health and morale.

But whatever avenues you explore, the main idea is to combine the two attributes of openness and discrimination as much as you can. There's no reason to feel grateful just because someone deigns to look your way. But, by the same token, there's no reason to turn up your nose at the short man with the specs and the funny last name just because he's not your romantic image of the ideal

Sometimes the natural need for love and understanding pushes the unmarried woman into brief relationships that she regrets immediately they are over. Even then, saying goodbye is not easy. At least it helps to know that women today are expected to make their own choices in matters of love.

lover. Short and nearsighted he may be; burdened with an almost unpronounceable last name he may be. But far more important, he may also turn out to be decisive, understanding, gentle, cheerful, and many other good things you wouldn't have dreamed of at first glance.

Sometimes it happens that you run into someone marvelous—even eligible—but somehow, nothing more develops between you than a solid friendship. If so—if he's someone you can really talk to, laugh with, and rely on—count your blessings. Indeed, to any woman already on her own, the benefits of having such a friend, or friends, hardly need explaining. No, we're not talking about friendships with homosexuals. They're all right as far as they go, but in the end, don't often do much for your morale. What we mean is that most rare and valuable relationship between a man and a woman: genuine friendship. If it has just a hint of something more to it, a "wouldn't it have been nice" feeling, all the better.

As you may have discovered, however, real friends of the opposite sex can be more difficult to find than lovers. So, if such a man, or men, comes your way, make the most of it. We can all do with that extra little sparkle that goes with relating to a member of the opposite sex, even on the most platonic level. Male friends can also be incredibly helpful when you're facing the myriad trials of making it on your own in a world whose financial, social, and psychological complexities are sometimes hard to master. More than that, men friends are simply entertaining, interesting, and comforting. Intimacy isn't everything, and the knowledge that you are liked, respected, and cared about by a friend of the opposite sex can mean a lot to you at all times, but especially in times of trouble.

Then there are those men who don't become friends or anything more, those passing fancies who come into your life, and just as suddenly disappear from it. Possibly because you want it that way, possibly

Being with a male friend who is not a romantic interest can be relaxing and comfortable—and still has an extra sparkle simply because he's of the opposite sex. When he's enough of a friend to help you out on bothersome financial problems, too, you're lucky indeed, and should appreciate it.

because they want it that way, possibly because you both want it that way, the relationship begins and ends in a matter of days or weeks. It may or may not have reached the affair stage, but anyway, you're not grieving over the loss.

What bothers you is that it happened at all, or that, despite the temporary boost to your ego, the net result is the kind of lost and disenchanted feeling we described earlier. What to do? Well the first thing to do is to stop worrying about it, and concentrate on something more important. Brief encounters of this type are a kind of learning experience, part and parcel of the larger experience of finding yourself alone and free. Many newly independent women, seeking to redefine themselves, their femininity, and their sexuality, go through a hectic phase of temporary relationships like these. For many, it's a necessary phase, a way of rediscovering their sexuality without the threat of becoming emotionally involved before they're ready to be. As their sense of security and self-confidence develops, however, they usually begin wanting a deeper and more lasting relationship.

Sometimes, though, a woman gets herself involved in fleeting, unfulfilling relationships not because she wants to, but because she

You're more than casually interested in a new man, and so you want the children to like him, too. It's delightful if you all get on well, and you can enjoy a family-like outing; but you must try not to let the children get too attached, because their hurt can be as strong as yours if the relationship ends.

doesn't know how to say "no." Perhaps she doesn't value herself highly enough, or perhaps she overestimates the vulnerability of the male ego, but whatever the reason, she finds herself saying "yes" when she'd really rather not. If so, it's time she brushed up on her brush-off technique. She doesn't have to be brusque or scornful, shocked or sarcastic about it. Retorts like, "What do you take me for, anyway" or, "This must be the tenth time this week I've been propositioned!" can produce uncomfortable situations. By contrast, a refusal as short and simple as, "Please, not so fast," or as sincere as, "I'm deeply involved with someone else and I just couldn't," or as honest as, "I'm not ready to be so involved yet," is both smoother and gentler. Yes, it's true that some men can't take any form of rebuff. But there are others who can—provided it's tactful—and still others who will be secretly relieved at not having to prove themselves. If your hesitancy is simply due to the fact that you'd like to know the person better first, and you say so, he's more than likely to give you that opportunity. If he's not willing to deepen the relationship before he asks you again, he's not worth worrying about anyway.

Finally, there is the real love affair. Some love affairs bloom suddenly, like exotic flowers, overnight. Others, like the song says, "just start quietly, and grow." But however it starts, and however long it lasts, a genuine love affair involves genuine feelings. You understand, care about, and need each other. You can talk and laugh together, share sad and silly things together, and, of course, make love together. If you enter into it heart and soul, you are naturally taking a risk. But generally, it's a risk worth taking, one from which you will both emerge, separately or together, richer people. Certainly, for many a newly single person, this kind of love relationship is as necessary as rain to a drought-parched land; it renews their capacity for loving—for feeling, giving, and receiving—both spiritually and physically.

There isn't much you can tell a person who is experiencing this kind of love affair. But there are two very valuable bits of advice, culled from Harriet LaBarre's book, *A Life of*

Your Own, that might be worth remembering. The first is to retain, despite your eager involvement, a certain amount of freedom, independence, and privacy. In other words, don't give up the key to your door, don't give up your own special friendships, don't give up your right to make plans and carry out decisions on your own. The second is to be just as honest as you possibly can be about marriage. If it's what you want, say so; if it's not what you want, say so; and if you change your mind about it, say so. Misunderstandings on this delicate, but important, score can lead to the greatest heartaches of all.

Finally—and this point is only for women with children—try to steer a course between candor and discretion. You need not keep your affections a secret from the kids, nor do you need to involve them in what are essentially adult matters. They can accept the idea that you are looking for someone to love, even that you have found someone to love, but it is far too much to ask them to accept signs of intimacy between you and the

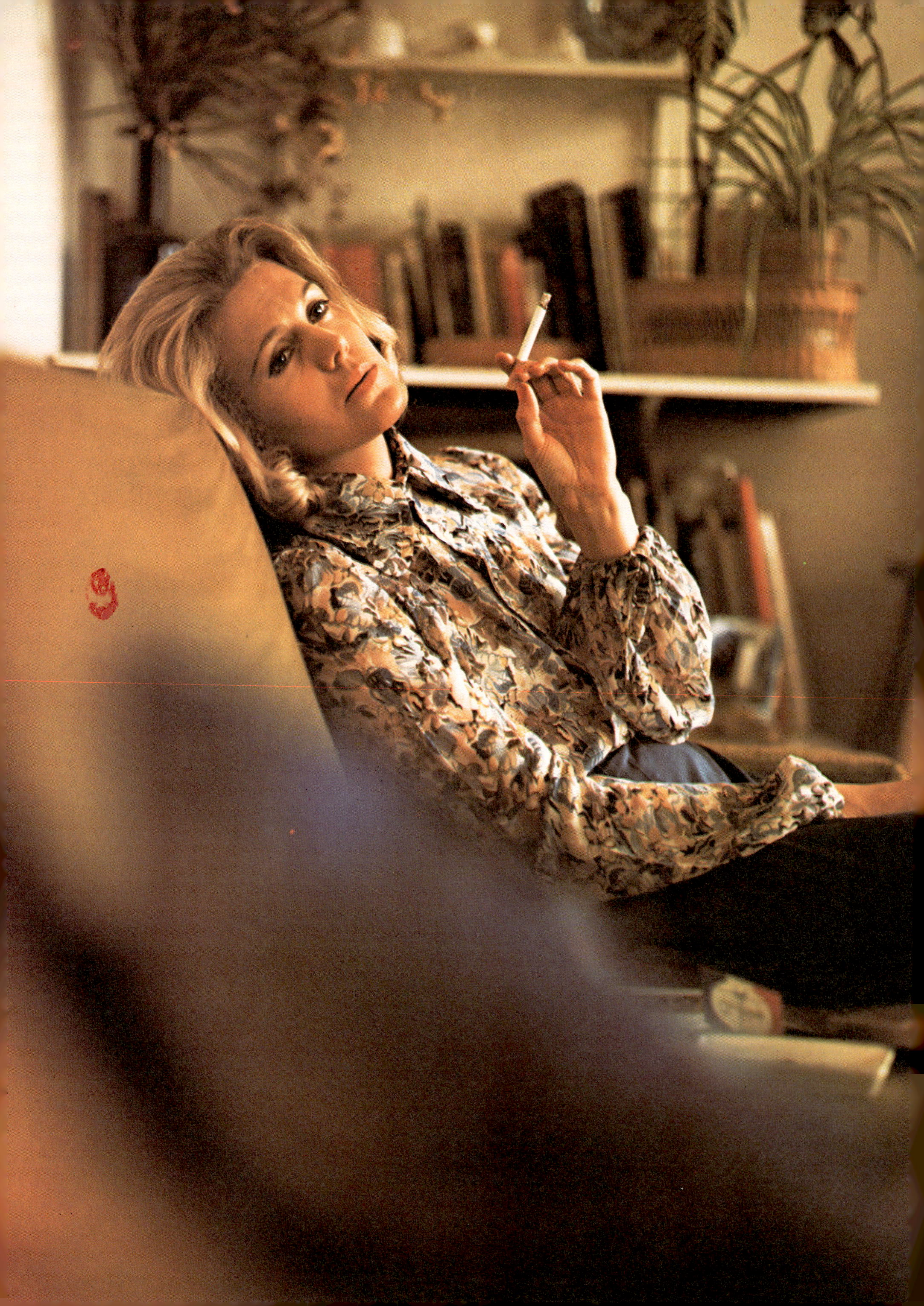

man you are in love with. If you possibly can, shield them from becoming too attached to him themselves. If the relationship ends, they will be just as hurt—if not more so—as you yourself are.

One kind of especially hazardous affair that many women alone embark upon is the affair with a married man. So much has been written on this subject that it's almost unnecessary to say more. Of course it's going to be fraught with all manner of limitations and sources of unhappiness. There's the need for secrecy, for example, the unavoidable jealousy of the woman he belongs to legally, and the uncomfortable, ever-present awareness of the clock ticking away. Worst of all is the near certainty that it will end. But, knowing all these things full well, many a woman goes right ahead and becomes involved with a married man anyway. "I know it's only going to last a short time," says one, "but I'd rather love him and lose him than not have him at all." "I don't think I could handle anything more than a part-time relationship like this anyway," says another, "so I can live with the fact that we'll never be able to get married."

Are these women deceiving themselves? For nothing is so painful as the loss of someone you love dearly, and it is impossible to be entirely prepared for it however much you know it may happen. Still, loss can occur in any relationship, even when the man involved is eminently eligible. So, yes. Possibly even considering the potential for unhappiness inherent in such a relationship, the choice remains each woman's to make for herself.

What do you do if and when a love affair ends? Well, first, if you're like most of us, you cry as though your heart would break. And why not? You feel it is broken. Then, if you have a close, supportive friend—either male or female—you go to that person and tell the whole sad story. You give way, quite naturally, to the bleakest form of self-pity, and regard the world with sadder, and not-yet-wiser eyes. In fact, a sort of mourning period is almost unavoidable if you cared a great deal about him, and just has to be lived through.

There are ways to make it better, however. One of these is to be realistic, and accept the fact that it's final. Trying to revive a relationship is a sure way to let yourself in for more unhappiness. Another, necessary thing to do is to keep busy. Concentrate harder at work, repaint your apartment, and plan a hectic social schedule that simply doesn't allow for many do-nothing hours alone. Finally, tell yourself as many times as you need to that, if you could love once, you can love again. Perhaps you will even be better at it next time, and perhaps the next man in your life will be better at it too.

There's no getting away from it, of course; the end of an affair usually hurts a good deal. But, as you begin to get over it, you may experience a curious feeling of release, even of relief. You're you, you're whole, and you've survived. "The best part of the whole ordeal," said one woman, "was when a friend of mine asked me if I were still seeing the penguin. I said, 'The *who?*', and she said, 'You know, Jake, the one who looks like a penguin.' At first I was furious. Barbara hadn't seen me for ages, and didn't know about me and Jake, but even so . . . Then, all of a sudden, I began to laugh. He did look like a penguin! I laughed until the tears ran down my face and Barbara began to look worried. 'What's up?' she asked. 'Oh, nothing,' I said, 'I just never saw him that way before.' You know, it was right then and there that I knew I was really over him!"

Perhaps your love affair doesn't end, however. Perhaps it just goes on getting richer and deeper and ever closer to the possibility of marriage. Will it last? Will you marry? How will it affect the children? These questions, so important to the woman on her own, we'll take up in the final chapter, "Where Are You Going?"

Sad, lonely moments are usually numerous in the life of the woman who chooses to have a relationship with a married man. The question to ask is: "Will the hazards and limitations be worth it?"

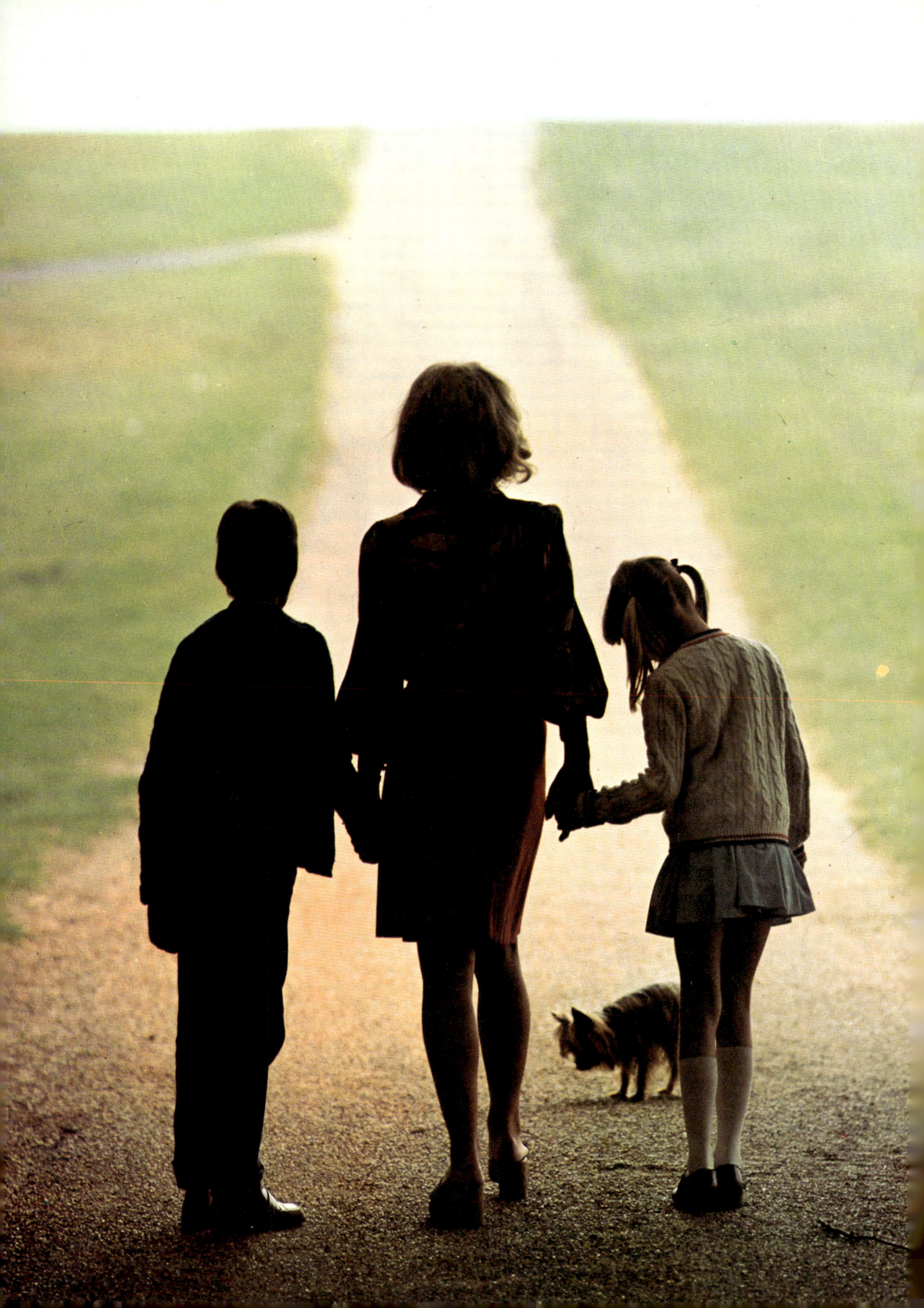

Where Are You Going?
8

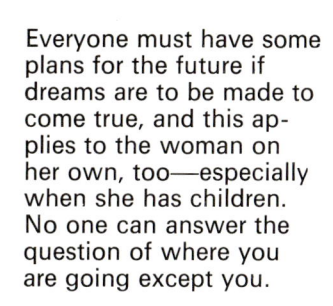

Everyone must have some plans for the future if dreams are to be made to come true, and this applies to the woman on her own, too—especially when she has children. No one can answer the question of where you are going except you.

Though marrying, or remarrying, may not be an overriding concern for every woman on her own, it certainly is for many—and with good reason. The very phrase "on your own" implies its opposite: the possibility of joining your life with another's in that most demanding and fulfilling of all relationships, marriage.

So what are the odds that you will eventually marry, or marry again? By all accounts, very high. Statistically, as few as three per cent of the women in this country remain unmarried past their middle years, and there are more single men than single women in every age group up to the age of 44. But that's just for first timers. No fewer than six out of seven divorced men and women eventually remarry, and most of them do so within a few short years after their divorce. Widows and widowers also tend to remarry at a fairly high rate, right up through—and even past—their middle years.

In fact, your chances of marrying a second time are much higher—at any age—than if you had never been married. A widow of 45, for example, is three times more likely to marry than a single woman of the same age. Two out of three women divorced at 40 will marry for the second time, while only one out of seven single women that age will marry for the first time. Even under the age of 30, the odds favor the once-married woman. Of those divorced by the age of 25, for example, 99 out of 100 women can expect to marry, as compared with 88 out of 100 women still single at age 25.

All of this clearly suggests that, if you have your heart set on marriage, you're fairly certain to get your wish—particularly if you've been married before, and particularly if that marriage ended in divorce. But why, you may ask, should so many people whose first marriages failed be so willing and eager to try again? Are they just basically the marrying kind? In a way, yes. In fact, most of us are, according to the statistics. Are they perhaps driven to it by the hard realities of living alone? Again, to some degree, yes.

Social pressures, financial pressures, and the children's need of a father, for example, can all play a part in a divorcee's wish to remarry. But there is an even more powerful motivating force behind the formerly married person's desire to marry again. That is simply the longing for married love.

It might be said that, once tasted, married life—and the potential for married love that goes with it—becomes almost irresistible. Marriage makes possible a kind of intimacy and emotional fulfillment no other relationship can match. Even when a first marriage was not a happy one, the man and woman involved have usually glimpsed its potential. This explains why, for the majority of formerly married people, love affairs, however exciting, remain basically unsatisfying. Both men and women feel the need to share the little moments in life as well as the big ones, the day-in, day-out details of living as well as the special occasions. They want to be loved and needed, understood and accepted just as much when they are rumpled and tired as when they are looking and feeling their best. Most of all, they want to share their future, whatever it is, with someone they trust and care about.

All this might be said of the still single person as well—with the significant difference that the single person has never experienced the total sharing that is part of married life. It has even been said that one of the reasons explaining the unmarried person's continued singleness is that essentially, they either do not want or do not need the real intimacy of marriage. A man or woman who has been married before, on the other hand, has not only experienced this need once, but is also likely to go on feeling it, and searching for a meaningful way to fulfill it.

This being the case, what are the chances that a person who has been married before will make a go of it the second time around? Again, amazingly good. Studies show that 75 per cent to 85 per cent of second marriages are happy and satisfying, even very happy and very satisfying. And although second marriages have a higher failure rate than first ones, no fewer than 60 per cent of them last until death.

This may come as a suprise, because most of us have grown up with the belief that if a person couldn't make a success of marriage the first time, they're almost bound to fail on the second attempt. Along with this notion goes the idea that divorced people all suffer from some sort of neurotic need that makes them fall for the same type of wrong person over and over. But both these views have recently undergone an overhaul. It's now clear, not only that second marriages have a good chance of success, but also that being

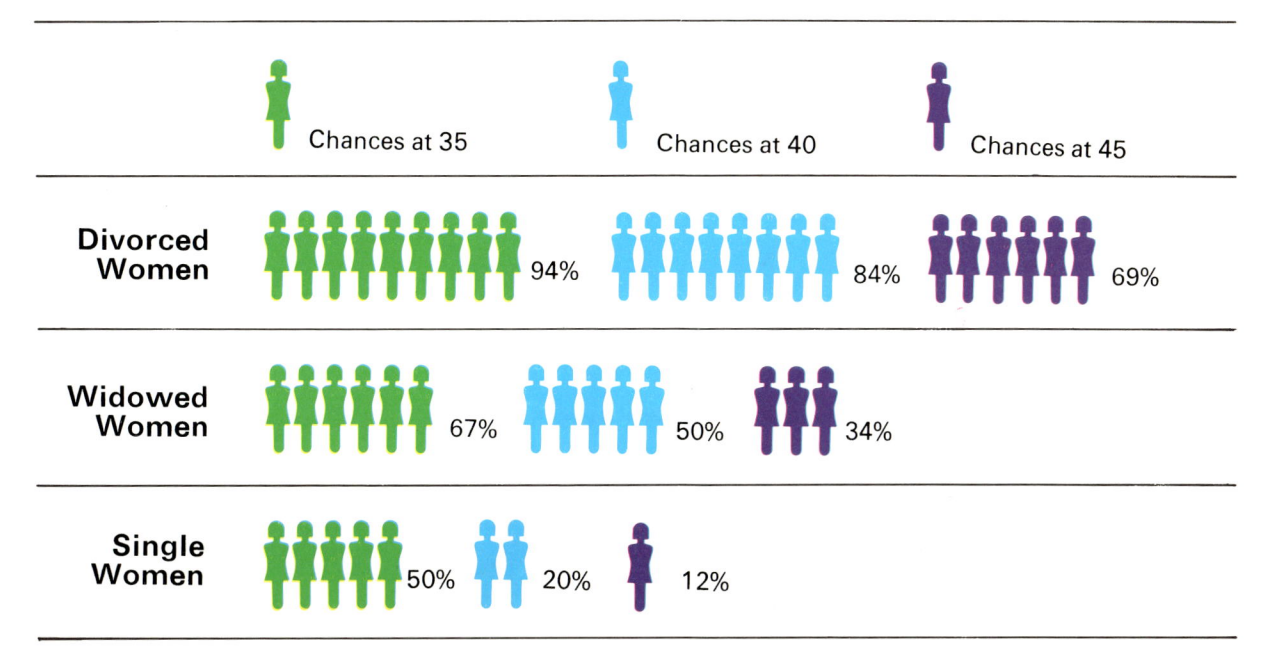

Left: you have found the man who has convinced you that it's worth trying a second marriage. This happy state of affairs can come about any time, and is no less wonderful later than sooner.
Below: this chart shows the high percentage of divorced and widowed women who marry again.

	Chances at 35	Chances at 40	Chances at 45
Divorced Women	94%	84%	69%
Widowed Women	67%	50%	34%
Single Women	50%	20%	12%

> The first wife, the first marriage—of course there are regrets and wishful thinking brought to mind by the old photograph. But you should not worry too much about being compared to his former wife. Most divorced men and women pick a new partner whose personality and character are much different from the old, and so avoid the same incompatibility.

divorced doesn't make you a person with neurotic needs.

It used to be thought that we are all just the products of our childhood, permanently stuck with our basic hangups and patterns. But the light is beginning to dawn. It's now being realized that we are actually capable of change, capable of learning from experience, capable of relating to new people in new ways. A first marriage, however unhappy, is a learning experience. So is its aftermath, living the single life. The proviso, of course, is that the person involved be ready and willing to learn—and the vast majority of formerly married people clearly are. Perhaps this is because the experience of divorce and living alone again usually makes such an impact on one's outlook and personality. Very few men and women emerge from this period of trial without having learned a lot about themselves, and the marriage behind them.

Often, when two divorced people meet and fall in love, they say to each other, "If only I'd met you before." But both of them know deep down that they might not have been ready to love the other before. In fact, the two people they have now become might never have existed had each not been through all they have been through. Both are more whole, more of a person, as a result of their experiences. They not only know themselves better, but they are also more sure of what they want, and what they can give to, this new relationship.

Perhaps it's this growth in personality that explains, more than anything else, why most divorced men and women do not marry a carbon copy of their first partner. They have come to see just why they were incompatible with their husband or wife, and perhaps have even ceased to blame them for what went wrong. Knowing their own needs better, they are more prepared to recognize the right person when he or she comes along.

Of course, there are a few men and women who neither learn nor change, but instead, tie themselves up once again with the same old problem type—another hopeless alcoholic, for example, or another heartless philanderer. But most formerly married people tend to steer clear of the type they already know will only make them unhappy, and seek instead a completely different kind of person. This change in goals—and the happiness that can result from it—is typified by the experience of Jenny Dowling, a tall redhead in her mid-thirties:

"My first marriage," she confesses, "was to a man who epitomized everything I thought I wanted. David was handsome, romantic, and full of boyish charm. But along with it went an incredibly childish temper, and a refusal to accept any kind of responsibility. He brought out the mother in me, but I soon found that I, too, needed someone to lean on, and he just wasn't there in that way. After five disastrous years, we were divorced, and another three years went by before I met Bill. I knew immediately that he was the man for me, and thankfully, he felt the same. We were married within six months, and I've never been so happy. No, he's not as handsome or as dashing as David, but he's warm and kind and steady as a rock. He's been divorced, too, and I guess that explains why we love each other with such tenderness and appreciation."

Jenny's second marriage, and the brief courtship that preceded it, illustrate other common aspects of love the second time around. As Morton Hunt, in *The World of the Formerly Married*, points out, not only do divorced people marry other divorced people 60 per cent of the time, but also their courtship tends to be far shorter than if they hadn't been married before. It's also true that their dating period tends to be characterized by a high degree of directness and domesticity. They usually begin making love fairly early in their relationship, for example, and, especially if one or both has children, begin early to try out the roles of husband and wife, mother and father.

Both know how important it is to learn everything they can about each other in all kinds of situations—alone together, with the children, with their friends—and they are eager to do so. They talk for hours, argue and make up, hesitate and recommit themselves.

All the time, they are engaged in the process of getting to know each other's tastes and temperament, habits and history, strengths and weaknesses. They find special ways to please each other, and begin to work out compromises in all kinds of areas—about food, sex, and friends, for example, and, of course, about how to deal with the problems of the children involved.

How does remarriage affect the children of either or both partners? Karol Hope, co-editor of *Momma*, a monthly magazine geared to the problems of single mothers, puts it succinctly when she says, "Instead of two personalities to figure out, you might have four or five to merge." She doesn't say it's easy; no one does. There may be tears and tantrums, possessiveness and criticism, some hostility, and a lot of jealousy. The older the children, the more likely they are to accept the new situation, of course. But it can take

The boy is moody, and the new father may find it hard to break through to make friends. It will take much patience and understanding, as well as time, to gain acceptance by the child of another parent—father or mother.

time and patience, particularly on the part of the new parent.

The wisest course, in the experience of most second fathers and mothers, is to take it slow, and allow the children to set the pace at which the new relationship becomes established. It's also wise to be prepared for all kinds of reactions. Sometimes, when there's a new father in the house, a child may feel hesitant and anxious about coming to love him for fear of betraying his real father. Just as often, however, the child decides that mommy's new husband belongs as much or more to him, and will feel jealous of the attention his new father pays to his mother.

But children are adaptable creatures, and often amaze their parents with the speed at which they do accept the new situation. One reassuring fact is that the children living with the custodial parent (almost always the mother) tend to be far more favorably inclined to her remarriage than to the remarriage of the visiting parent (almost always the father). Studies also show that the most important factor influencing a child's attitude toward his mother's remarriage is her own attitude toward it. In other words, if she quietly asserts her right to love and marry again (rather than anxiously promising the child that he'll always come first in her affections, or placing a lot of the responsibility for her decision on his young shoulders), he is far more likely to weather this change in his life in a healthy and natural way.

One question that often arises when a remarriage occurs is: should the children be adopted by, or change their last names to that of the new father? This is a controversial point, probably best solved by the individuals involved. Certainly, changing a child's name to match that of his new father, his mother, and future brothers and sisters may add to his sense of belonging. But it should be remembered that changing his name—especially when his real father is encouraged to give up legal responsibility for him—is also a way of subtracting from his unique identity, his own personal story. What's in a name? A good deal, unfortunately, and this kind of decision must be thought about with the greatest care. Even psychologists do not agree on the subject, but one thing is clear: neither mother nor child should see the changing of their name as a way of sweeping divorce under the carpet. It has happened, and perhaps the greatest lesson of all is that it is not their names so much as their capacity for growing, changing, and forming wise and happy relationships that matters.

Thus far, we've been speaking mainly to the woman with marriage on her mind. But you may well be one of the many women who wishes to remain single—at least for the time being. Perhaps you are simply enjoying your new freedom too much to tie yourself down again. Or perhaps, for you, it's still a question of "once bitten, twice shy." Alternatively, your first marriage may have been so fulfilling and harmonious that it's become a hard act to follow. Perhaps you feel that marriage just isn't right for you right now. Or perhaps it's simply a question of your not yet having found the right person.

But whatever your reasons for remaining single at present, you probably want to know more about what's in it for you. We've already touched on some of its possibilities: being able to make your own decisions and choose your own friends, for example; finding challenge and satisfaction in your job; being able to play the role of single parent with ingenuity and pride; finding self-expression and renewal through love. Are there still other possibilities? Yes, and lots of them.

To begin with, there's the immediate world around you—your city, neighborhood, and community. Yes, we've already touched on the possibility of joining activities and groups for the fun of it, and to meet new people. But there's another facet to this kind of participation, one that is perhaps even more important. That is giving, caring, and making some contribution to the society you live in.

Now we're not suggesting that you become a saint, and devote yourself heart and soul to one demanding crusade after another. What

With her virtually unlimited freedom of action, the single woman has a unique opportunity to serve the wider community. It may be lobbying for more low-cost housing, consumer protection, or other needed social change by door-to-door canvassing. It may be by working with children in formal organizations, such as the scouts, or informally in a club formed for special activities. It could be group social work for the elderly, or the handicapped. There's so much that needs doing—and you'll gain, as well as give, by your involvement.

we are suggesting is that you, as a single woman, are in a unique position to give, and to gain from, becoming involved with the world around you. Making a positive contribution to the lives of others has a way of adding dimension, purpose, and meaning to your own. Because you know and value yourself, because you believe that what you do with your life is important, and above all because you are a free agent, it may be possible for you to make that kind of contribution. You certainly don't have to look far to see what needs doing. The problems of women on welfare, youngsters in trouble, lonely handicapped children and elderly people, not to mention the crying need for new protective legislation of all types (the preservation of our environment is just one

She feels that living on her own is a good way of living for her, and she's an interesting person because she's interested in the world around her. Should she marry, she'll merely be adding another dimension to her already satisfying and full life.

example)—all these and many more issues need committed individuals ready to give of their time, their talents, and their energies. Why not be one of them?

Secondly, and a bit more selfishly, what about the world beyond your everyday experience? Namely, other places, other peoples, other parts of the globe. Single women simply don't travel enough. There are thousands of places to go—beautiful, exciting, relaxing, enlightening, touching, bewildering, glamourous, stimulating. Not all of them are expensive to visit. There are all kinds of package deals available these days. You can go with a group, you can go with a friend, you can go by yourself. In fact, in the experience of countless single women, both younger and older, who have traveled alone, you *should* go alone if you want to get the most out of it. But the main thing is to go. Who knows, next year you might get married, and not be able to take off exactly when, where, and how you choose.

Finally, what about your own inner world? America, perhaps more than any other country, is a nation of self-explorers. Sometimes we take it too far, of course. But carried out with a sure grasp of what is important and what is not, exploring the person you are, and want to be, can be the most rewarding journey of all. It doesn't have to be done with the help of psychoanalysis, group therapy, or encounter groups, though many single people find one or another of these experiences challenging and beneficial. All it requires is a questing mind, and an interest in what your particular life is all about. It's the kind of self-examination that can turn up all kinds of downright intriguing questions about yourself that need answering.

Try asking yourself, for example: "What is it that I really like doing, really enjoy? What kinds of things have I always promised myself to learn or to do that I've not yet been brave enough, or organized enough to do? What kinds of people do I really enjoy? Do I make opportunities and find time to be with them? What opinions, values, and convictions do I really hold, and why? Where do I want to be ten years from now, and what do I want to have accomplished?"

It would probably be overwhelming to ask yourself all these questions at once. But everyone must ask themselves where they are going at some point in their lives, and should go on asking themselves again from time to time. For the woman alone, the time is now. Because she, more than others, holds her life in her own hands, she, more than others, must know what she's doing with it. And, if possible, she must have some special, personal goal in life other than that of simply getting married.

If a woman's life as a whole, single person has meaning and direction, then marriage becomes yet another means to an end, rather than an end in itself. Married or single, a woman must be whole. It is only out of that wholeness that she can create a full life for herself alone, or a truly happy and successful life with another person. "Am I happy now that I'm married?" says a woman quoted by Patricia O'Brien in *The Woman Alone*. "Oh yes, but I'm not happier. I was already happy." Could there be a better testimony to the value of learning to live and grow on your own?

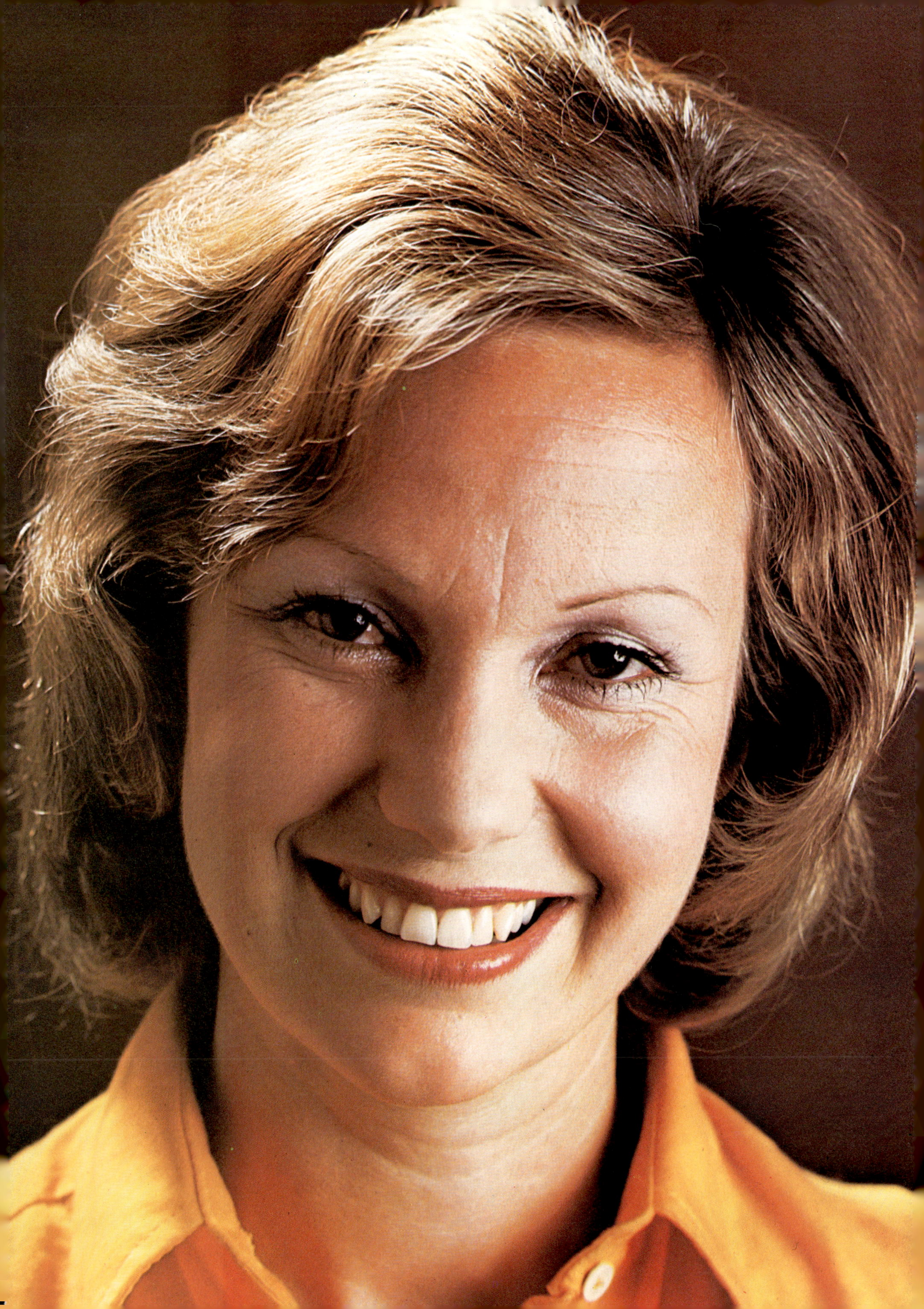

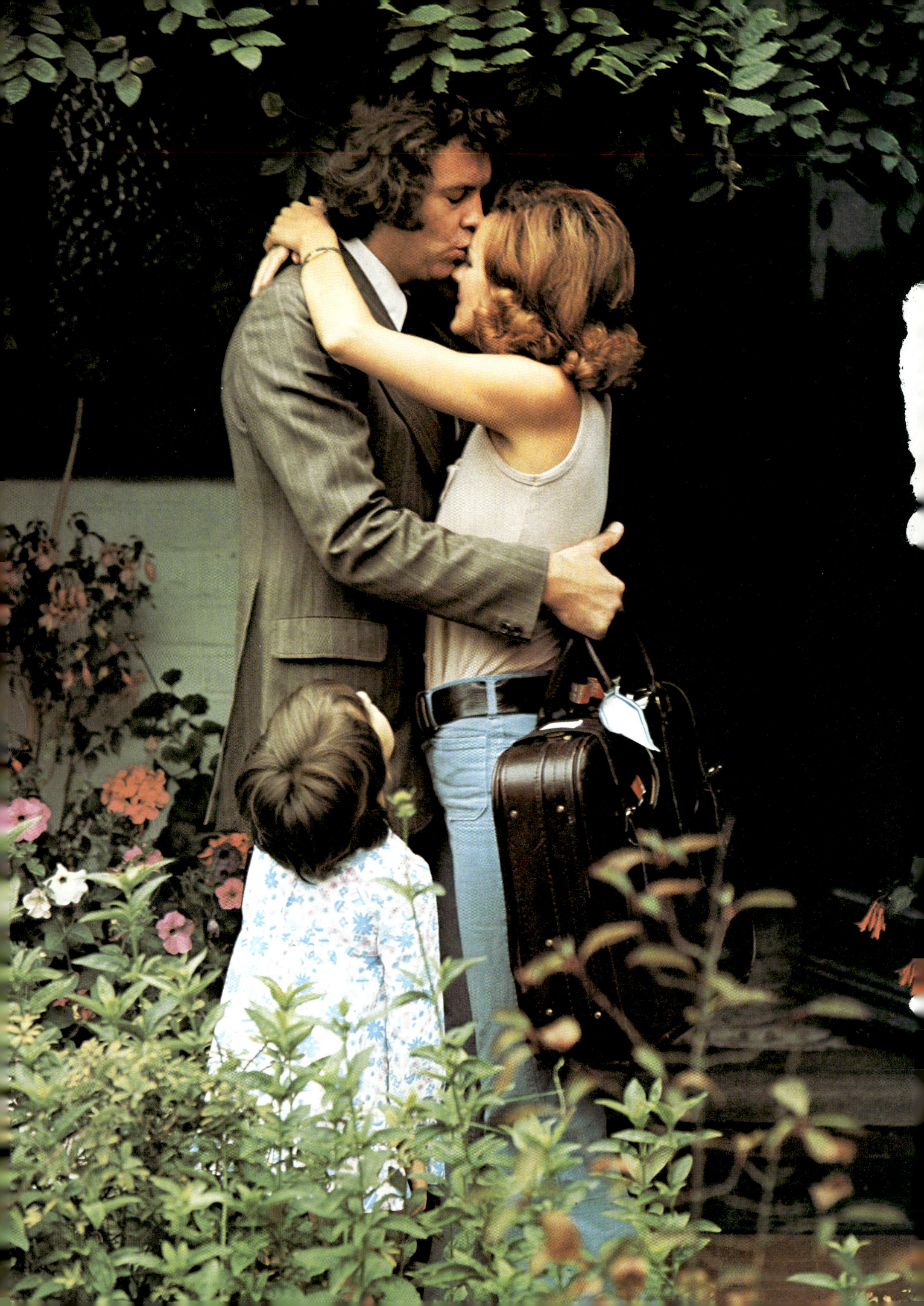

Questions & Answers

Thus far, we've been discussing the problems of the woman who is on her own as a result of divorce, widowhood, or remaining single. It's also possible, though, to find yourself on your own for still a different reason: simply because your husband is away. Perhaps he's doing his stint in the armed services, for example. Or perhaps he has the kind of job that requires long and frequent business trips. Or, more worrisome, perhaps a bout of illness makes it necessary for him to spend some time in the hospital. Whatever the reasons for a husband's absence from home, it can bring unexpected problems and challenges for his wife. On a short-term basis, and possibly on short notice as well, she may have to take over as full head of the household—with all the headaches and responsibilities that that may entail. What is it like to find yourself temporarily on your own in this sense? What kind of problems can it pose for a woman as wife and mother? A few of the more common ones, together with some real-life examples, are discussed in the first part of the question-and-answer section that follows.

The next part of the supplement deals with the ever-present problem of money. Certainly, personal finances are a matter of concern for almost everyone these days. But for the woman alone—especially if she is relatively inexperienced in financial matters, or if she is trying to manage on limited resources—the whole issue of money can become an overwhelming problem. The questions and answers in this next section cover some of the things that may be worrying her—from support payments on divorce, and benefits under Social Security and Welfare, to taxes, investments, credit ratings, and information on the drawing up of a will.

The final part of the supplement is devoted to a matter of vital concern to every woman who is on her own—for whatever reasons and for however long. This is the problem of personal safety: exactly what precautions should be taken to safeguard her person and property (both inside and outside the home), and what to do if she has reason to feel her safety threatened in any way.

He's off again—the husband whose job takes him frequently away from home—and you're left to manage the house and family. This means that, though married, you have a lot in common with the single woman. So this book is for you, too.

When He's Away

My husband's engineering firm has just promoted him to a job that entails working abroad for several months each year. It's a big step up for him, and naturally I'm proud of his success, but the thought of the long separation worries me. Won't it tend to weaken our marriage?

Not if your marriage is basically sound to begin with. Countless thousands of couples endure separations lasting months—even years—without the essential strength of their relationship being altered one bit. In fact, unavoidable separations of this kind often serve to make the bond between husband and wife even stronger. Having to be apart can help each to realize how much they love and need the other, and how much their life together really means to them.

Nevertheless, it's perfectly natural to feel distressed and anxious at the prospect of a lengthy separation. After years of being together every day, it's a little like being thrust back into the uncertainties of courtship days. How will the two of you react to being apart? Will the physical distance between you create an emotional distance as well? Will it be harder to communicate when you're back together? Suddenly, the man and the marriage you've come to take a little bit for granted become especially valuable, and you become more aware of how important they are to you.

In many ways, of course, this kind of realization is a good thing. If the prospect of a separation moves you from a state of complacency to one of greater appreciation, the marriage as a whole is bound to benefit.

It may also help to remember that a separation of this kind is no worse than many other stresses and strains you'd expect a marriage to weather. Among these might be having an elderly relative live with you, experiencing financial difficulties, uprooting the whole family to live in another part of the country, or seeing a child through a period of illness or trouble. Part of being married, of course, is taking the bad with the good. Separation is no exception. If your relationship is founded on love and trust, the ties that bind will not come loose, however far apart you may be geographically.

All this, of course, isn't to say that being separated isn't difficult for both partners. Apart, both are necessarily thrown more on their own resources, and are likely to become more aware of their own individuality, strengths, and weaknesses. It can come as a jolt to have to function separately when you are used to functioning as a team. This is an aspect of separation that may not dawn on either partner until they actually find themselves on their own.

My husband is a sales representative, and has to spend weeks at a time traveling. He always tells me how much he's thought about me and the children, but I wonder if he really misses us as much as we miss him.

Most wives whose husbands travel a good deal have felt this way at one time or another. They feel that when a man is away working and traveling, he's too busy and preoccupied to miss his family much. This line of thinking assumes two things: first, that a man has to be within sight of his family to think about them; and second, that his life away from them is particularly exciting and fulfilling. For most men, neither of these things is true.

Let's look at it from a man's point of view. In most instances, it's the demands of his career that take him away from home. He may be a serviceman doing a long tour of duty, for example. Or a salesman who has to spend a certain amount of time in the field. Or a businessman who is regularly asked to make trips abroad. In none of these cases is he likely to have the high life his wife might imagine. To take the first example of a serviceman, spending months on a Navy cruiser, constantly surrounded by other men in uniform, can hardly be described as easy living. As for salesmen and businessmen, who has not heard them bemoaning the soullessness of the hotel rooms they have to stay in? It is a classic complaint, and it sums up the kind of depersonalization they often feel away from home.

In fact, it's when the working day is over that a man can feel most lonely and in need of his family. After being surrounded by strangers most of the day, and probably still feeling weighed down by the responsibilities of his job, it can be very depressing to have no one to come home to, no one who really knows him or cares about him. "Glamorous, it definitely isn't," says one man whose job entails frequent trips abroad. "When I'm away, I miss everything—even the fights my wife and I sometimes have. You can't argue with a hotel TV set, let alone kiss it good night!"

The truth is that most men miss their wives, their children, and their homes far more than we give them credit for—sometimes even more than they will admit.

A man may get lonely away from home, but doesn't a wife get even lonelier? She's the one who's left behind, after all.

It depends, of course, on the kind of person she is, and the kind of relationship she has with her husband. However, an unavoidable separation can indeed be harder for a woman than for her husband. She remains in the familiar surroundings of her home, but without the familiar presence of the man who helps to make it her home. He has new places, new people, and new challenges to take the edge off his loneliness. She has not, and when she is used to a life of day-to-day sharing and interdependence, a sudden and prolonged separation can come as a jolt to her.

Jill Baker, a 34-year-old mother of three, describes the experience this way:

"When Jim announced that his company was sending him on a series of three 6-week training sessions, I wasn't too upset. In fact, I looked on it as an ideal opportunity to do some redecorating because I actually like doing it, while Jim hates it—especially when it turns the house upside down. Imagine my surprise when I found myself really depressed over his absence. We'd never been separated before in seven years of marriage, and I more or less did an emotional swan dive. I felt too tired to do anything I'd planned, and yet at night I found it hard to go to sleep because he wasn't there beside me.

"That was how it was for me the first time he went away. The second time wasn't so bad. I threw myself into painting and papering, and worked like a zombie until he returned; but I still didn't feel like myself. It really wasn't until his third trip away that I learned how to change gears, pace myself, and carry on solo without feeling like a wounded bird. What it all made me realize is not only how much I love my husband, but how much I'd come to rely on him to supply an emotional security, and give structure to my life. Now I'm glad I've had a chance to prove that I can function alone when I have to."

Letty Dahlbeck was faced with a different and graver problem when her husband went away. A helicopter pilot on a tour of duty in Vietnam, he was in serious danger most of the time, and Letty lived in a constant state of anxiety. Nonetheless, she schooled herself to carry on as normally as possible. "You have to," she says simply. "Otherwise you'd go off your rocker. At first I was so terrified for him that I could hardly think of anything else. But gradually, I realized that my obsession with his safety couldn't help him. Certainly it wasn't helping our little boy, who picked up my anxiety, and became nervous and fretful. So I steeled myself to adopt a fatalistic attitude. If a permanent separation was what fate had in mind for us, there was nothing to do but wait, and pray, and accept that might happen. Thankfully it didn't. Bruce came home safe and sound at last, and it now seems like a nightmare of long ago. But it certainly has made me a stronger person in every way."

Not many wives, fortunately, have to face such a grueling test of endurance. But a large number do have to live with the kind of on again-off again situation in which their husbands are frequently away from home for a week or more at a time. Darlene Vesco's husband, for instance, is away ten days every month. "I've long since adjusted to being a once-a-month widow," she says, "and you know, I actually get a kick out of it. While Ted's away, I indulge myself by letting the house go a little bit, slopping around in any old comfortable clothes, staying up late reading, and fixing just the simplest, easiest meals for me and the kids.

"Then, when he's due to return, I rush around like a whirlwind, making me and the house look beautiful, and fixing a special dinner. The first night he's home, the kids get to stay up later, and then he and I sit down to have a long talk, and catch up on what's been happening. I really look forward to his coming home, and so does he. It makes a celebration out of just being together—kind of a once-a-month honeymoon. Frankly, it does our marriage a lot of good, and I wouldn't want things any other way."

Besides the emotional impact of being apart, what specific problems might a woman have when she's temporarily on her own?

It seems that women in this situation run into certain common problems, and the kind of trouble she might have usually falls into one or the other of three categories: social, financial, and parental.

Socially, if her husband is away for some time, she may run into a curious situation—that of feeling that she's neither married nor unmarried. Though her friends may rally round her at first, with invitations coming fast and thick, they may begin to stop being so concerned about her after a while, and leave her out of the usual marital gatherings. After all, even if only on a temporary basis, she is a woman on her own—with all that implies. It often comes as a shock to a married woman to realize that she can be a bit uncomfortable with her married friends, and they with her. Here she is, not only alone and missing her husband, but also feeling somewhat stranded as a social being. There really isn't much she can do about the situation except grin and bear it—after all, it won't last forever.

One thing she can do, though, is avoid those tricky situations that divorcees, widows, and single women are only too familiar with: namely, looking like a prime target for a proposition. Husband away? Heavy jobs and repairs that need doing? Alas, the combination can provide the perfect setup for an offer of help that becomes more than an offer of help. "You could have knocked me over with a feather," says June Felsen, "when my neighbor's husband began making passes at me. He'd only come over to help me fix the washing machine, but it didn't take long for me to realize that he figured I was in need of 'company.' I was furious, especially when he told me that I shouldn't have asked him in if that wasn't what I wanted."

The only way to protect yourself from being taken advantage of in this way is to make it clear that you're not looking for flirtation just because you're on your own. "I play it very light and cool when my husband's away," says one woman. "For one thing, I don't do the 'helpless female' bit—if I can't fix something myself, I get a repairman to do it for me. Also, I avoid problem situations such as driving home with a friend's husband after we've had a few drinks, for instance. Not only my marriage, but also my friendships, mean too much to me to put them in jeopardy."

Another problem that may confront the woman who is on her own for a period of time is the business of money. If her husband has the kind of job that takes him away regularly, she and he will probably work out a system of bill payments that either means he takes care of it when he's home, or she handles it in his absence. But there are situations in which a wife suddenly, and for a long period, has to take over fully.

Supposing a man unexpectly has to go into the hospital for lengthy treatment, for example. More than one wife has found herself not only experiencing the anguish of worry about a sick husband, but also facing a pile of bills and regular financial commitments she knows nothing about. It can be unnerving, to say the least, to discover that you must take over this responsibility when you are completely in the dark about your mortgage and insurance payments, banking arrangements, and credit situation. If and when a woman finds herself facing this problem, and her husband is too ill to be consulted, she must simply roll up her sleeves, and, by going through her husband's records, discover for herself exactly what financial commitments must be met. If necessary, she may have to put herself directly in touch with the bank, insurance company, and so forth, to find out where she and her husband stand. In most cases, she will find the individuals she has to deal with both understanding and helpful.

Of course, it's far better to know about these things in advance. In far too many marriages, the husband doesn't bother to explain the family's financial position to his wife—nor does his wife show any real interest in this side of their life. This may seem like the easiest way of managing things, but it's just asking for more trouble if trouble comes your way. Every wife should be ready and willing to learn all the details of the family's financial setup (even if she hates anything to do with figures, clauses, and contracts) just in case she ever has to take over temporarily. Among other things, being in the know will make her feel far more of an equal partner in the marriage.

Finally, there is the parental problem: dealing with the children effectively when their father is away. For some reason, many children become more difficult to handle when their father is absent for an extended period. Perhaps it is because they feel that the whole domestic setup is threatened; certainly, the younger they are, the more difficult it is for them to adjust to the idea that daddy is away, but is coming back. Perhaps, too, it is because they feel the need to test their mother's strength in this new situation. Whatever the reason, it can be an extra burden for a woman to have her children being especially hard to handle when her husband isn't there to lend his support, and back her up in disciplining them. In this respect, again, a woman temporarily on her own is in a similar position to the young widow or divorcee. As a mother, she has to provide her children with the reassurance that their lives are going to proceed as usual, despite the absence of their father. The best way to provide this reassurance is to stick to the normal routine as much as possible, and insist on the same standards of behavior as she would when the children's father is at home. Doing this—like coping successfully with any of the other problems we've discussed—can add immeasurably to a woman's sense of confidence in herself, and, incidentally, can give her a deeper insight into the problems of the woman more completely on her own.

Financial Problems

On being divorced, I was awarded a certain amount each month toward the support and maintenance of myself and our three children. It's not a lot to begin with, and I now discover to my worry that I have to pay taxes on it. Can this possibly be right?

Yes, unfortunately. To see why, you have to look closely at the wording of your separation agreement. When it is agreed that a husband will contribute to the support of both his wife and his children, and *no differentiation is made* between how much is for her and how much for them, the two sums together can legally be considered alimony. Because all alimony is tax deductible by the person paying it, the person receiving it is responsible for paying the taxes on it.

To avoid this, the amount a wife is awarded in addition to what is awarded for her children should be carefully differentiated. An agreement of the right kind might read: "The husband agrees to pay the wife the sum of $2000 annually for the support and maintenance of herself, and the sum of $2800 for the support and maintenance of the children." In this instance, he could deduct the $2000 he pays to his wife, but not the $2800 he pays for his children.

If, however, the agreement reads: "The husband shall pay to the wife the sum of $4800 annually for the support and maintenance of herself and children," he is entitled by law to deduct the entire amount from his gross income before taxation. Since somebody has to pay the taxes on this money, it therefore becomes the wife's responsibility. Though the hardship this creates for the wife may not have been the intention of the agreement, it certainly is the effect. This is one of those cases in which the exact wording of a financial arrangement can have unexpected and long-term repercussions.

After a divorce, which parent is allowed to claim the children as dependents?

Child support (which, increasingly, is the only form of regular payment awarded to the wife) is not deductible from a husband's gross income before taxes. He is, however, permitted to claim the usual deduction for each dependent, including himself, when computing his taxes. In some cases, the husband agrees to let the wife claim the children (in addition to herself, of course) as her dependents when paying her taxes. When nothing at all is agreed between husband and wife on this matter, the rule is that the person who contributes 51 per cent of the children's support is the one permitted to claim them as dependents.

My husband is making a good deal more now than when we were divorced. Is it possible to have the amount of his support increased?

Some separation agreements include what is known as an "escalator clause." Such a clause will state that, if and when the husband earns more than the amount he was making at the time of the divorce, he will agree to pay a certain percentage more of his earnings toward the support of his children (and of his wife, if she is to receive support as well). But even where there is no escalator clause, it is often possible for a wife to obtain an increase in the support payments based on a significant improvement in the husband's earnings. This is especially true when she is acting on behalf of her children only. But whether she is acting for them alone, or for herself as well, she will have to take the case to court unless her separation agreement already includes an escalator clause.

Which of the two divorced parents is responsible for the children's medical costs?

In most separation agreements these days, the husband assumes the responsibility for carrying a basic health insurance policy for his children. In many agreements, the husband also makes himself liable for all "extraordinary medical costs" not covered by the basic policy—special hospital and surgical expenses, for example. This only makes sense, of course, because normal support payments would not begin to cover the astronomical expense of special medical treatment these days. But when it comes to "minor" medical expenses, the husband is not considered to be responsible unless he so chooses. Fillings and broken arms, medicines and treatment for common childhood illnesses—these costs must be met by the mother out of the support money she receives. To add to all this, in many cases she also finds herself having to pay the bill for any orthodontic work needed to straighten the children's teeth. This last is a controversial subject because, despite the cost, some husbands take the line that orthodontic work of this kind is not an emergency, and so does not come under the "extraordinary medical costs" they are liable for.

How does a wife's remarriage affect the amount of support money she receives from her husband, and the question of who claims the children as dependents?

Any support money the wife has been receiving for herself stops, of course, when she remarries. But, as most separation agreements specify, the husband's responsibility to contribute to the support of the children continues as before. As to the question of who claims the children as dependents, it depends on who is paying 51 per cent of their support. If, despite her remarriage, the main contributor to their support is still her former husband, he is permitted to claim them as dependents. If her former husband is now contributing less than 51 per cent of their support, she is the one who claims the children as dependents.

For the first year after our divorce, my husband made his support payments fairly regularly. Then he began to get behind, and finally stopped payments altogether. Now I understand he has left the state. What can I do?

Sadly—and infuriatingly—this is a situation countless thousands of divorced mothers find themselves in. For every responsible ex-husband, it would seem, there is at least one irresponsible one. As long ago as 1956, in a book called *After Divorce,* William J. Goode reported that 51 per cent of divorced men made the support payments ordered by the court either rarely or not at all. In this respect, things haven't changed much since 1956. Irregular payments and partial payments, checks that bounce, and husbands who simply disappear—all these problems are with us just as much as ever, and perhaps even more so, because the divorce rate keeps going up.

So what does a woman do when the money she needs to pay the rent and buy the family's food and clothing doesn't arrive? She can go to her lawyer to bring the case to court, of course. But her lawyer will probably advise her to wait until the sum owed to her becomes big enough to be "worth suing for." How much is that? Usually something between $1500 and $2500. So, before she can take it to court, she will probably have to wait a good while. (She will also have to find some way to manage in the meantime.) If and when the sum becomes big enough to be worth a lawsuit, she is more than likely to be told that the only way it can be recouped is by having her husband's salary attached. This is done by a legal action in which a certain amount is automatically deducted from a person's salary check to pay off a debt. Unfortunately, a large number of businesses and corporations take the view that a person with an attached salary is a bad risk. The fact is, they often fire a person when notified that an attachment has been made against him.

Obviously, a man out of a job, like a man who has been jailed (which is another punitive action that can be taken against a husband for nonpayment) is not going to be able to make any payments whatsoever. This being the case, the wife involved has very little option but to forgo the money owed her. The only benefit of threatening to take legal action is that in some cases it may scare the nonpayer into making payments.

What if a husband leaves the state? If his wife plans to take action against him for nonpayment, she must first find him. To do so, she may have to hire a private detective, which, of course, is another expense. An interstate statute can be invoked against the husband, once he is found. But it may take some time for this to come into play, by which time he may have gone to yet another state. If this happens, the wife will have to begin all over again from scratch.

If all this sounds like a pessimistic view of a wife's chances for recouping what is owed to her, it must be said that it does represent the findings of many legal advisors as well as many distressed wives. In fact, the widespread incidence of nonpayment is one of the reasons why so many women are not only going back to work, but also demanding better pay. With seven million American families headed by women, and many of those women having to make do without the support payments awarded them, work—and well-paid work—becomes a necessity. As one divorced mother tells it: "The struggle for my children's support payments took everything out of me, and produced nothing but empty promises. In the end, I just gave up. I know my ex-husband feels guilty about the situation, but that doesn't pay the rent. I do. And believe me, it's a struggle keeping the three kids and myself fed, clothed, and decently housed. But in one sense, anyway, I've been lucky. I may not have support payments to depend on, but I do have a good job. For all our sakes, I intend to keep it."

I am divorced and facing a financial crisis. I've been ill off and on for a year, and have had to give up work temporarily. I have two children. Are we eligible for welfare benefits, and how do I obtain them?
Yes, you are eligible, under the federal Aid to Families with Dependent Children program. AFDC, as it is called, is administered by the individual states, and is designed to provide money, medical care, and social services to families with insufficient funds to meet their needs. The state agencies administering AFDC go under such names as the Department of Public Welfare, the Department of Social Services, etc., and your first step is to contact the department office nearest you. There, a social worker will ask you to fill out an application and answer various questions to determine the size of the grant you are eligible for.

What kind of questions will they ask?
The majority of questions will pertain to your present financial position. You will be asked whether or not you are working, and how much you earn; whether or not you are receiving support payments or other regular contributions from relatives, and how much they amount to; whether you rent or own your home, and how much rent or maintenance you pay; whether or not you have a car, and what its cash value is; whether or not you have savings in the bank, and how much;

and, of course, how many children are in your care, their ages, and whether or not they are in school. (In many states, children are eligible for AFDC benefits up to the age of 21, but only if between the ages of 18 and 21 they are regularly attending high school or college, or taking a vocational or technical training course.) You may be asked to furnish various documents, like the children's birth certificates, as verification of the statements you give. You will also be asked to notify the agency immediately if any change takes place in regard to your earnings, living arrangements, property holdings, etc.

How does the welfare agency arrive at an assessment of how much you need? In other words, how much might a mother of three get from welfare?
The assessment of need is approached differently by the welfare agencies of the different states. Some states have a definite ruling on how much can be awarded for the parent, how much for the first child, how much for each child after that, etc. Other states do not specify any maximum amount. But despite this variation, one thing holds true: generosity is not the rule. However much the tax payer bemoans the welfare system, he cannot accuse it of making life easy for those it's supposed to help. Eight out of 10 welfare recipients are women and children in dire need. Yet in most cases, what they receive in welfare benefits is barely enough to keep their heads above water. It's worth noting that, as of 1968, the official definition of poverty for an urban family of four was an annual income of $3535. Yet even in states with no maximum ceiling on AFDC benefits, a woman alone with three children is not likely to get more than $2800 a year.

Will the welfare agency deduct from their assessment any child support from an ex-husband?
Yes, if it's above a certain sum, and regularly received. A typical instance was that of a woman in Washington, D.C. who was out of work, but receiving $200 a month in child support from her ex-husband. As a woman with three children, she was eligible for a monthly welfare grant of $238.50. But because of the child support she was receiving, she got only $53.50 a month in welfare.

Supposing a woman works, but cannot make enough to support her family. Will her earnings be deducted from her welfare grant?
Up to a certain point, yes. Even a job that pays very little can affect the size of the welfare check, and often, the proportionate deduction means that the person's total income, despite working, is less rather than more. This is one of the major controversies surrounding the whole issue of welfare today. Welfare agencies urge their clients to seek training and employment outside the home, but the problems this can raise for a hard-pressed mother are monumental. Public funding for day-care centers is minimal so far, and even the most understaffed and ill-equipped center can cost a woman as much as 45 per cent of her gross income. Though some 75 per cent of all welfare mothers have worked at jobs outside the home for most of their adult life, they find themselves unable to make enough to support the family, and pay for day care, without supplementary benefits. Yet those same supplementary benefits are reduced in proportion to their earnings.

What can you do if you feel that your welfare agency is giving you less than you are eligible for?
There are two things you can and should do. The first is to find out what your full rights are. This can be difficult, admittedly. The administration of welfare is characterized by so much red tape and officialese that even welfare workers sometimes find it hard to sort out all the various rulings that may apply to a specific case. This is just one reason why the National Welfare Rights Organization was founded. In this growing association welfare mothers are pooling their individual knowledge and experience to help one an-

other obtain what they are eligible for, as well as lobbying for legislation that will help, rather than hinder, the mother alone.

Even without turning to the national organization, you may learn some valuable information by discussing your problems with other welfare mothers. Where complicated welfare rulings are concerned, two heads are often better than one. When there are six or seven or more of you, the combined knowledge of the group may produce a solution that none of you alone might have thought of. Mutual help and solidarity of this kind can do a lot to raise morale.

Getting to know your rights is not the only thing you can do, though. Even if you are unsure about whether the action taken by the welfare agency is correct, it's wise to ask for a hearing. "If you are dissatisfied with the action taken," reads the general information leaflet put out by a typical state welfare service, "the county agency will review it with you. If you then believe that you should not have been denied aid, that your application did not receive prompt or proper consideration, or that you are eligible for a larger grant, you have a legal right to a review hearing. The county agency or regional office of the State Department of Health and Social Services in your area will assist you to request a review hearing."

Welfare clients in all 50 states have the right to a hearing—without charge. The state agency involved must grant it, and, if the client is in the right, the agency may give in quickly. After all, since it means calling in the agency lawyer, a court reporter, and the particular social worker involved, it's expensive to drag it out, especially if the law is on your side. In an amazing number of cases, the law *is* on your side.

Is it true that people not currently married pay 20 per cent more in taxes?
Yes it is. Before 1969, when legislation was passed on this issue, single people paid as much as 40 per cent more than married couples. But even with the amount reduced by 20 per cent, the tax bias in favor of married people is still pretty sizeable. In point of fact, 30 million single Americans pay $1.6 billion more in taxes every year than married couples. (It should be noted here that anyone is considered single for tax purposes if he or she is not supporting dependents. This means that many widowed and divorced people, as well as never-married people, are paying the higher, single tax.)

As things now stand, there are four separate tax tables: one for single people; one for heads of households; one for married couples filing jointly; and one for married couples filing separately. There's a movement afoot now to set up a uniform tax structure for all taxpayers—married, single, widowed, or divorced. A tax structure like this would not penalize anyone, whatever their marital or domestic setup.

How are credit ratings determined? Are credit standards higher for women?
Credit status, which is a deciding factor in getting loans, mortgages, and retail credit, is determined by the following criteria: the amount you earn, and the permanence of your job; where you live, and whether you rent or own your home; your past bill-paying record; your assets (savings, investments, life insurance, etc.); and finally, your age and marital status. Most wage earners and bill payers are listed at their local credit bureau, which stands ready to supply verification of their credit status when they apply for bank loans, mortgages, leases, etc.

At present, credit practices tend to work against single women, widows, and divorcees. All three are considered a greater financial risk than a single, divorced, or widowed man, and a much greater risk than a married man. Women alone, however much they earn, are generally required to meet higher standards than men to get the same credit rating. Often, too, when a loan or a mortgage is involved, they must have a male co-signer to obtain it. Even when a woman has worked throughout her married life, she can find herself with a zero credit rating if the marriage ends; the credit goes with the husband.

These prejudicial practices are now under attack all across the country. Twelve states have already passed legislation to equalize women's status in obtaining mortgage loans, and one state (Washington) has passed legislation prohibiting sex discrimination in all forms of credit and financing.

I'd like to begin investing as a hedge against inflation. I'm by no means rich, though. Would it be too much of a gamble?
Investing does entail risks, but you can reduce some of the gamble if you're prepared to educate yourself on the subject thoroughly and carefully. While you will want and need a trustworthy broker, you should not place yourself trustingly and unquestioningly in such hands. Instead, make it your business to learn the basic facts about stocks, bonds, and mutual funds. It's not easy, but it can be done. As a start, you might want to go to the library and read an article in the June 1973 issue of *Ms.* magazine, called "How the Small (Very Small) Investor Can Make the System Work for Her." Among other things, it includes a chart listing various types of investments according to their income safety, and appreciation value. But don't stop there. Get one of the many good beginner's guides on the subject, and learn about the profit and risk aspects of various investment alternatives.

When considering investing, several points should be kept in mind. First, don't plan on committing any more money than you can afford to *lose*. Second, be sure you know what you want out of your investments. If you want rapid growth with the possibility of a quick profit, for example, you will have to sacrifice the element of safety. If, on the other hand, you want to be sure of a steady income of interest or regular dividends, you will have to forgo the chance of rapid gain. (One way you might get the best of both alternatives is to put your money in the kind of mutual fund that spreads its investments over different types of securities, and seeks to achieve a balance between steady income and capital gains.) Third and finally, before you invest a cent, test yourself as an investor. Choose your stocks or bonds, follow their progress in the daily market reports, and keep track of how much you would be making—or losing—if you actually had money in them. This is an excellent way to try out your knowledge without risk. Remember, whether or not you use a brokerage or a mutual fund, your knowledge will remain a prime factor in making sure investments suit needs.

How can I figure out how much Social Security I will receive each month when I retire?
The amount of the Social Security check you are entitled to after retirement age (62 for women) is based on two factors: the number of years you have worked by then; and your average earnings over the years. Where the first of these two factors is concerned, it's important to note that the *year* you reach 62 plays a role in determining whether or not you are fully insured. The farther ahead your 62nd birthday, the more years of working credit you need—up to a point. If, for example, you reach 62 in 1975, you'll need credit for six years of work. But if you reach 62 in 1991 or beyond, you'll need credit for no more than ten years of work. It's also important to note that having the necessary years of working credit only serves to make you fully eligible for Social Security benefits. It does not determinate the size of these benefits. The specific amount is determined by your average earnings over the years.

Your Social Security office will, of course, figure the exact amount of your benefits when you file your application with them shortly before retirement. But long before that time you can arrive at an estimate of how much you will receive by following the steps in a handy little pamphlet called *Your Social Security*, put out by the Superintendent of Documents, U.S. Government Printing Office, Washington, D.C. 20402. This pamphlet will also tell you about Medicare and disability benefits; how much you can earn while receiving Social Security; payments to your dependents in case of your death; and the benefits available to dependent widows, children, and surviving divorced wives. This pamphlet is not only very informative, but very clearly written. It's well worth having now, whatever your present marital and working status.

My husband suffers from a heart condition, and I know I must prepare for the worst. I don't want to distress him, but I feel that for the sake of myself and our children, I should begin to educate myself about our financial position. Is this advisable, and if so, how should I begin?

This is indeed a wise step to take. It is, in fact, what every wife should do, even if her husband is in perfect health. Preparing for the possibility of a husband's death takes courage and foresight, but death does inevitably create financial and legal problems. Unless a wife prepares for them, with the help of her husband, she can find herself facing a host of bewildering difficulties when she most needs peace of mind.

You ask how you should approach this problem. There couldn't be a better way than to read something about the legal and financial facts of widowhood. One of the best books on the subject—clearly written and easy to understand—is Luis Kutner's *How to Be a Wise Widow*. Learning in advance about the kind of things you might want and need to ask your husband will make your discussions on the subject easier for both of you. You will be in a better position to understand his affairs, and he will therefore be more able to explain them.

Each individual case is different, of course, but there are a few musts that apply to everyone. The first is that there should be a will, carefully drawn up with the help of a legal advisor. A will accomplishes several things. It states how a person wishes to distribute his assets (cash, real estate, securities, personal belongings, business interests, etc.) It gives instructions for the payment of debts, the expenses of a last illness, and the cost of the funeral, burial, and memorial services. It may also provide for the creation of special trusts for dependents. Finally, it designates a competent executor.

It should be noted that a will does not go into effect automatically on a person's death. It must first be subjected to probate, an official investigation carried out to determine its authenticity. It must then be administered, a process that entails appraising the assets of the estate, and paying all accumulated debts. Only then can the net assets be distributed according to the will. All this can take anywhere from nine months to two years. Because the money held in a joint bank account can be frozen during this time lag, it is advisable for emergency money to be held in a separate bank account for the wife.

Two final words of advice: a wife should not only thoroughly understand her husband's financial and legal affairs, but should also know where he keeps all the relevant documents—the will, life and health insurance policies, birth and marriage certificates, safe deposit box keys, securities, real estate records, military discharge papers, Social Security Card, employment records, copies of tax returns, and bank account records. All these can play a crucial part in simplifying the paper work that goes with sorting out a widow's position. In addition to knowing where these important documents are kept, a wife should have a list of trusted friends and advisors familiar with her husband's affairs to whom she can turn in an emergency. Among these should be his lawyer, accountant, banker, insurance agent, investment counselor or stock broker, and doctor.

The points we have covered are, of course, only a few of the things a wife ought to know. It cannot be stressed enough that every wife should acquaint herself with her husband's financial and legal position. It is not being grim to prepare oneself for the worst. It is simply common sense, and a responsibility every woman owes to herself, her children, and even her husband.

Personal Safety

I've just begun living alone, and my friends seem bent on scaring me with stories about burglars and prowlers. They tell me I've got to learn to live "more defensively." But I just refuse to cower in my corner like a frightened rabbit. Isn't all this talk of crime being exaggerated anyway?

No it isn't, unfortunately. Even the most innocent looking surroundings can prove dangerous these days, and it's unwise to imagine that any area you live in or travel through is perfectly safe. Living in a perpetual state of alarm, of course, is equally as unhealthy as throwing care to the winds and taking unnecessary chances. But you can't go wrong by recognizing potential dangers, and doing what you can to safeguard yourself against them. Statistics show, for example, that a woman on her own is at greatest risk when she is out walking, driving, or in her own home. Of the three, the area she has most control over is her home, and there is a great deal she can do to make it safer.

What basic precautions should I take to minimize the risk of a break-in?

Clearly, the first priority is to have good locks installed on your doors and windows, and then *use* them. Surveys show that as many as one in six people go out leaving their windows open, and even their front door unlocked. The kind of lock you get is also important. Two of the most burglar-resistant types are the double lock and the dead-bolt lock, though there are some other excellent nonspring locks available too. It's vital to change the lock on your door when moving into a new house or apartment; you never know how many keys may have been made to fit the old one. A chain guard on the door, and securely fitting window locks, are also essential. You may want to get a locksmith to advise you about these safety devices, and install them for you. If so, make sure he's a bonded locksmith, and don't begrudge the cost. It's worth every penny.

Another precaution you should take is to use only the first initial of your given name with your surname when listing yourself in the phone book, and on your mailbox. Why tell the world you're a woman living on your own? For instance, B. for Barbara could just as easily be B. for Bob or Brian. You might even want to add another name—one you just make up—under yours on the mailbox. The more people who appear to be sharing your roof, the better—and the safer for you as a woman alone.

What other precautions should I take where my home is concerned?

There are a number of things you can do, some obvious, some not so obvious. Hardly anyone these days needs to be told how unwise it is to open the door to strangers—salesmen, repairmen, window cleaners, etc.—unless they have an appointment, and can show an identification card. On the other hand, many a woman alone needs to be reminded how risky it is to use an apartment house launderette at night. Even though it's situated in her own building, it can still be a dangerous place to be alone in the evening.

Again, hardly anyone needs to be told how important it is to keep the phone numbers of the police, fire department, hospital, and ambulance service taped to the phone, or next to the phone, in case of emergency. But it may be less obvious how important it is for a woman to establish useful contacts with her neighbors, and also with her building personnel, if she lives in an apartment house.

Security experts recommend that a woman alone find a trustworthy neighbor (preferably one who's often at home), or her building superintendent—or both—to keep a special watch on her place. Where building personnel are concerned, a generous Christmas tip can help encourage cooperation. Where neighbors are concerned, a readiness to return the favor can create a valuable mutual support system. ("I'll look out for you if you'll look out for me.")

In a more general sense, it might be said that if there's safety in numbers, there's also safety in being *known* by numbers. In other words, don't be a loner. No woman should live a life of shadowy anonymity just because she's on her own. The spirit of neighborliness isn't dead, even in our biggest cities. (Witness the birth of tenants' associations and neighborhood councils all over the country.) Get to know your neighbors—and also your mailman, local grocers, dry cleaner, etc.—by name as well as by sight. Let them know you in the same way. Even this much contact will make you more a genuine part of the community—and in that sense of community lies greater security for everyone involved. You know them, they know you, and should anything go wrong, there's much more chance that someone will be aware of it, and do something to help.

Supposing you wake up in the night and find that someone has broken in, and is prowling around inside your home?
Everyone hopes and prays that this will never happen, of course, but if it does, security experts recommend one of two courses of action, depending on the kind of home you have. If it's a house, and you can possibly get out a back door or window quietly, do so, and go to a neighbor's to call the police. If it's an apartment, or you can't get out of the house without risking an encounter with the prowler, the best thing you can do is to stay in bed, and pretend you're still fast asleep. This takes nerve, but remember that the overwhelming number of break-ins are for purposes of burglary, pure and simple. The risk of personal harm arises if and when the burglar thinks he's going to be caught at it. So stay quiet, and let him take whatever valuables he can find. It's safer to raise the alarm when he's gone.

How do you deal with obscene phone calls? One of my friends has started getting them, and she's terrified to answer the phone.
It's precisely this kind of fear—and revulsion—that the makers of such calls delight in creating. So the first thing to do in combatting this kind of attack is to refuse to be intimidated. Inform the caller, coldly and firmly, that you are reporting the call to the police, and to the phone company. Then waste no time about doing so. When reporting the call to the police, repeat what has been said to you word-for-word, even if you feel you can't bear to. This is important, for one of the ways such callers can be identified and traced by the police is by the particular line they take when making phone calls of this kind. As for the phone company, it has developed sophisticated methods for tracing such calls.

What special precautions should I take when going out alone in the evening?
When you go out, it's wise to leave your radio or television on, and at least one light burning in a room you'd be likely to be in—your bedroom or living room, for instance. If you live in a house, don't go away leaving only your front porch light on. This

is a clear signal that you are out for some hours.

When invited out for the evening, try to make sure there's an escort lined up to see you home. If this isn't possible, it's usually better to take a taxi, rather than a calculated risk, on your way home. Expensive? Yes, but more than worth it if the alternative is a lonely journey by public transport, followed by an equally lonely walk from the bus stop or subway station to your front door.

When you go home by taxi, have your door key ready, and ask the driver to wait until you're safely inside. If you live in an apartment building, and have to take an elevator, don't get into it with anyone who looks even remotely suspicious. This word of advice also applies to any other time of day.

Finally, as you approach the front door, or step inside, if anything at all looks suspicious to you—such as the door being improperly locked, a light out, or a window open—don't go in alone to investigate. It's foolhardy to tell yourself that you might have left things that way in your hurry to leave. Maybe you did, maybe you didn't. The important thing is not to take any chances. Even if it's late, get someone else to go in with you, and check things out.

What precautions should be taken when I'm out walking, especially in the evening?
First, stick to busy, well-lighted streets. Second, walk closer to the curb than to the buildings you pass. Third, try to vary your route slightly from day to day. All three will minimize the risk to yourself.

What if I'm being followed?
If it's by someone on foot, cross to the other side of the street. If you are still pursued, run to a lighted house or shop, and call the police. If it's by someone in a car, turn around and run in the opposite direction. The driver will have to make a U-turn to follow you, and the time this takes him will give you an opportunity to run for a lighted residence or business.

What if I am suddenly accosted?
If he demands your purse, hand it over—and have at least a few dollars in it. Desperate thieves have been known to turn on their victims if there's no money in the purse or wallet they demand. If, however, your attacker is threatening you personally, start screaming, and keep on screaming even if he orders you to stop. He may run off if there's a chance someone will hear you. As terrible as it is to think of it, there are situations in which a woman's best chance of survival is to give in. Because this is a choice no woman wants to make, any potentially dangerous situation should be avoided.

What precautions should I take when out driving alone?
Always stick to busy, well-lighted streets. Travel with your car doors locked, and your windows rolled up, and leave your car in gear at stop lights and school crossings. Try not to allow your car to be forced off the road by another vehicle—even if it has flashing red lights—unless it is a clearly marked police car, ambulance, or fire vehicle. Neither should you stop if another motorist signals that there's something wrong with your car, or that he has broken down. It is better to drive to a service station to have your car checked, or to send help to the motorist in distress. If you ever have reason to think you're being followed by another car, don't drive home. Make for the nearest police station, or busy service station, instead. Finally, if you're driving home after dark, it's always better to park in the street, rather than to drive into a dark garage.

What should I do if my car breaks down in an isolated area?
Raise the hood of your car, and turn on your emergency blinkers. Then get back inside, keeping your doors locked, and your windows rolled up. If another car or a passerby stops, open your window slightly, and ask for assistance to be sent to you. Do not get out to talk to those who stop, and on no account accept a ride from them.

For Your Bookshelf

The World of the Formerly Married
by Morton M. Hunt, McGraw-Hill Book Company (New York: 1966)

A Life of Your Own
by Harriet LaBarre, David McKay Company, Inc. (New York: 1972)

Why Isn't a Nice Girl Like You Married?
by Rebecca E. Greer, The MacMillan Company, Collier MacMillan Canada, Ltd. (Toronto: 1969)

The Woman Alone
by Patricia O'Brien, Quadrangle/The New York Times Book Company (New York: 1973)

How to Be a Wise Widow
by Luis Kutner, Dodd Mead & Company (New York: 1970)

Raising Your Child in a Fatherless Home
by Eve Jones, The Free Press of Glencoe, The Macmillan Company (New York: 1963)

When Parents Divorce
by Bernard Steinzor, Pocket Books, Simon & Schuster, Inc. (New York: 1970)

Explaining Divorce to Children
edited by Earl A. Grollman, Beacon Press (Boston: 1969)

A Complete Guide for the Working Mother
by Margaret Albrecht, Doubleday & Company, Inc. (New York: 1967)

The Case for the Working Mother
by Dorothy Whyte Cotton, Tower Publications (New York: 1965)

Picture Credits

Aldus Archives 12(BR); © Aldus Books 55, (Ann Dunn) 22(L), (Mary Tomlin) 48-49, 119, (Photos Dmitri Kasterine) 68, 78(T), 95(T); Courtesy Austin McConnell Associates 130; Jim Bamber 32; The Bettmann Archive 40; Bibliothèque Nationale, Paris 13(TR); By permission of the Birmingham Museum and Art Gallery, Cover TC, 9(TR); Aufnahme Kunst-Dia Verlag Joachim Blauel München 6(T); From filmstrip 174.6 (French Costume) MS. e. Mus. 65, ff.99ᵛ. Bodleian Library, Oxford 12(BL); Reproduced by permission of the Trustees of the British Museum 10(T), (R.B. Fleming © Aldus Books) 7(BR), 11(BL), (Michael Holford Library Photo) 10(BL), (Photo courtesy Thames and Hudson Ltd.) 12(TR); Photos Mike Busselle and Richard Hatswell © Aldus Books, Cover R, 2, 4, 16, 28, 31, 33, 36, 44, 57(R), 58-59, 77, 79, 85(TC)(BR), 86-87, 89, 97(TR), 103-106, 114, 116, 118, 122-123, 124(T), 125, 127, 128, 134, 141; Camera Press (Lawrence Schiller) 26, (*Brigitte*) 18, 62-63, (*Sport*) 97(TL), (*Vital*) 52-53; The Cleveland Museum of Art, Delia E. and L.E. Holden Funds 14(BL); Colorific! (D. Dryhurst) 109, (H. Gritscher) 113; *Daily Telegraph* Colour Library 9(B); Capitoline Museum, Rome/Photo C.M. Dixon 60(T); Mary Evans Picture Library 13(B), 34(L); FPG., Cover TL, BL, 46(B), 80(BL), (Alan Felix) 51, (Hallinan) 23, 39, (Pastner) 15(BR), (William Simpson) 80(BR); Gallerie della Accademia, Venice/Photo Ferruzzi 13(TL); Henry Grant, A.I.I.P. (London) 46(T), 47(T), 64-67, 97(BR); Susan Griggs Agency (Julian Calder © Aldus Books) 70-71, 75, 83, 110, 111, (Anthony Howarth) 90-91, (Adam Woolfitt) 47(B), (Ian Yeomans) 80(T); By permission of The Huntington Library, San Marino, California 8(BR); India Office Library & Records/Photo R.B. Fleming © Aldus Books 8(BL); Magnum Photos (Rene Burri) 11(BR), (Burt Glinn) 11(TR); Mansell Collection 60(B); © Marshall Cavendish Ltd. (Photo Jerry Harper) 121, (Photo John Seymour) 85(TL); Metro-Goldwyn-Mayer Inc. 37; The Metropolitan Museum of Art, Bequest of Gertrude Stein, 1946 7(TR); Musée du Louvre, Paris/Photo Giraudon 8(T); Stadtisches Suermondt Museum, Aachen/Photo Matzkowski 15(TR); The National Gallery, London 14(T); National Portrait Gallery, London 6(BR), 41(R); PAF International 99(T); *Radio Times*/Photo Dmitri Kasterine 19(R); Rijksmuseum, Amsterdam 14(BR); By courtesy of The Marquess of Salisbury/Photo John Freeman 7(TL); Piero della Francesca/Scala, Florence 6(BL); *Sunday Times* Colour Magazine 97(BL); Syndication International 19(L), 56, 61, 82, 85(TR)(BL), 92(T), 97(C), 101; The Tate Gallery, London/Photo John Webb © Aldus Books 94; Three Lions, Inc. 38, 72-73, 124(B); Transworld 99(B), (Gerry Cranham) 35, (*Ladies' Home Journal*) 21, 92(B), 93(R), (*Observer*) 46(C), (Tony Peagam/*Observer*) 24, 25(L)(R); Hans Rudolf Uthoff/BFF, Colorvision International 43; Victoria and Albert Museum, London/Photo John Webb © Aldus Books 15(BL); The Walker Art Gallery, Liverpool 10(BR).